The Ballgame of Life

Lessons for Parents and Coaches
of Young Baseball Players

Standing Ovations for *The Ballgame of Life*

A practical guide for parents and coaches interested in teaching young athletes the game of baseball while remembering to remain positive role models themselves—both on the field and in life.
                                        —David Hansen, Major League Ballplayer

Finally someone stepped to the plate and wrote the book we have needed for many years. The Ballgame of Life *teaches parents and coaches of young ballplayers not only why they need to keep things in perspective when it comes to youth sports...but also how they can do so without taking the fun out of the game.*
  —Peter Ueberroth, former Commissioner of Major League Baseball

The Ballgame of Life *does a great job of guiding parents and coaches in how to teach children the best way not only to enjoy the great game of baseball but to take the lessons learned and apply them to their everyday life. It is a "must read" for those searching for the most effective way to get the most out of their baseball experience with young ballplayers.*
                              —David Magadan, Major League Ballplayer and Coach

The top professionals in the game all learned to play baseball right, and this is precisely what Joey Aversa and Dave Smith have tried to get across to parents and coaches of young baseball players in this book. The Ballgame of Life *is about the kind of early training that makes some of the past and present major league players special for many more reasons than their statistics. The odds of any ten year old becoming a major leaguer are a million to one, but it doesn't mean that he or she can't learn the same lessons about integrity, the joy of competition, and the value of team relationships that great players learned when they were ten.*
                              —Peter Gammons, ESPN Baseball Analyst
                              Member, National Baseball Hall of Fame

The Ballgame of Life

*Lessons for Parents and Coaches
of Young Baseball Players*

David Allen Smith and Joseph Aversa, Jr.

Foreword by Peter Gammons

The Ballgame of Life
Lessons for Parents and Coaches of Young Baseball Players
by David Allen Smith and Joseph Aversa, Jr.
with a Foreword by Peter Gammons

Edited by Gregory F. Augustine Pierce
Cover design by Tom A. Wright
Text design and typesetting by Desktop Edit Shop, Inc.

Cover art from a photo of a sculpture at the varsity baseball field of Augustana College in Moline, Illinois. The image is used with permission of the donor. The artist's identity is uncertain.

Published by ACTA Sports, a division of ACTA Publications, 5559 W. Howard Street, Skokie, IL 60077 (800) 397-2282 www.actapublications.com

Library of Congress Number: 2006920999
ISBN 10: 0-87946-299-X
ISBN 13: 978-0-87946-299-4
Printed in the United States of America
Year: 15 14 13 12 10 9 8 7 6
Printing: 10 9 8 7 6 5 4 3 2 1

About the Authors

David Allen Smith is an attorney and former American Arbi-
tration Association judge specializing in employee contracts and
sports transactions. He is the author of *From the Prom to the
Pros* and the father of one son.

Joseph Aversa, Jr. was drafted by the St. Louis Cardinals in
1990 and has over fifteen years of professional baseball experience, including coaching and instructing players from tee-ball
through the major leagues. He is a husband and father of two
sons.

Contents

Batting Practice / 11
Foreword by Peter Gammons

Warmups / 15
Introduction

Opening Pitch / 17
The Starting Lineup

First Inning / 19
The Goal of Every Great Coach and Parent

Second Inning / 31
Your Limited Window of Opportunity

Third Inning / 41
The Main Jobs of Parents and Coaches

Fourth Inning / 51
Success (and Failure) Leads to Success

Fifth Inning / 61
Developing a Healthy Definition of Winning

Sixth Inning / 73
Finishing What You Start

Seventh Inning / 85
Team, Teammates, Teamwork

Eighth Inning / 95
Know Your Players, Not Just Their Names

Ninth Inning / 107
Final At-Bats for Parents and Coaches

Extra Innings / 119
Ten Commitments by Parents and Coaches

Post-Game / 123
Acknowledgments

Box Score / 126
"True Story" Bylines

This book is dedicated to our fathers—Joseph Aversa, Sr., and Merlyn Lee Smith. They not only coached us in baseball and fatherhood, but their kindness, guidance, wisdom and patience also prepared us for the many other challenges life continues to pitch to us daily.

Batting Practice

Foreword

Distinguished author John Grisham spent tens of millions of dollars building a baseball complex out of the woods south of Charlottesville, Virginia, in the foothills of the Blue Ridge Mountains. He did so "out of a love of the game, and the desire to give kids of all ages in the area the opportunity to play, learn and improve."

Grisham mowed and lined the fields of the near-dozen diamonds himself. He charged only $25 for an annual fee, but if a child could not afford the $25, Grisham paid it himself. If a child could not afford a glove or shoes, Grisham found a way that the child could get them and play.

There were, however, rules. To start with, the only bleachers where parents could watch were in dead center field. "This is about the kids," Grisham said. Arguing with umpires or cursing of any kind were both banned. "Civility," said Grisham, "is not a bad thing."

It was the pure baseball dream of a very good man who loves the game of baseball and the way it should be played. And it can be played right—not by doctrinarian writ taught on video by some guy in Florida who believes everyone must do every-

11

thing *his* way (a way that would try to change a Miguel Tejada or mechanize a David Ortiz, their *duende*, their pure joy in competing), but by playing with a modicum of respect for the game and for one's peers.

The great George Brett once was asked how he wanted his career to end. "I want to hit a hard ground ball to the second baseman," replied Brett, "bust my tail down the line, and be out by an eyelash." No self-aggrandizement, just leave the game playing it the way it should be played.

One scout covered Hall-of-Famer Robin Yount for nearly ninety games in a five-month period. The fastest the scout timed Yount getting to first base was 3.9 seconds. The slowest was 4.0 seconds. "What is so hard," Yount once asked, "about going as hard as you can four or five at-bats a game?"

"That is why Robin is a Hall-of-Famer," says Yount's former teammate and longtime major league stalwart B.J. Surhoff.

Joe Torre says Henry Aaron is the only player he ever knew "who never made a mistake. He ran hard on every ball. He was the best base runner I ever saw. He ran perfect angles to fly balls, always was in position to throw, and never missed a cutoff man. He also was always the perfect gentleman, the perfect teammate." Aaron also is one of the four or five best players who ever lived, not to mention the all-time home run king. Because of his treatment in a segregated minor league world in the early 1950s and the treatment he received breaking Babe Ruth's home run record, Aaron could have become a totally different person, but he never changed from the man he was.

A baseball team is a microcosm of society, and teams work best—like society—when the last is treated like the first. In September 1978, when the Boston Red Sox were in the process of blowing a fourteen game lead over the Yankees, twenty-game winner and Hall-of-Famer Dennis Eckersley of the Sox loaded the bases. With two out, Yankee Lou Piniella hit a popup into right center. Five Boston players took chase. Despite being called off the play, utility infielder Frank Duffy—playing second because of an injury to regular Jerry Remy—had the ball hit him in the back.

Error, Duffy. Eckersley did not last the inning. Yankees 7, Red Sox 0. The Red Sox lead in the standings was down to one game.

Afterwards, the media surrounded Duffy. The rest of the Boston players were hiding in the trainer's room.

Out came The Eck. "Leave him alone," he screamed, pulling at writers. "He didn't load the bases. He didn't hang the 0-2 slider. He doesn't have the 'L' next to his name. Talk to me—the losing pitcher."

That moment remains the greatest example of being a teammate I have ever seen. Yes, Eck is in Cooperstown, and a year after that incident Duffy was out of the majors. It did not matter. Frank Duffy was Eckersley's teammate.

Baseball is about overcoming adversity: Willie Mays began his career 0-for-24. It's about discipline: Albert Pujols studying film and honing his swing so that when he goes to the plate each day he thinks only about what the pitcher throws. It's about looking in the mirror: Eckersley being the perfect example.

Baseball should be joyous. Every day Ernie Banks would say, "Let's play two." Miguel Tejada runs out onto the field 162 games a year, then goes home to the Dominican Republic and plays most of the winter because, as he says, "What could be more fun?" That energy that Derek Jeter, Derrek Lee, David Ortiz, Jeff Francoeur, Grady Sizemore and Vladimir Guerrero bring to their teams every day makes those teams better, because every other player feeds off them.

These players treat everyone—from teammates to clubhouse attendants to reporters to fans—with respect. In my thirty-five years covering the major leagues, no person has been more respectful to me than Mariano Rivera, the greatest reliever who ever lived. "We will all be judged by the way we treat others," says Rivera. "Respect others, and they will respect you."

The top professionals in the game all learned to play baseball right, and this is precisely what Joey Aversa and Dave Smith have tried to get across to parents and coaches of young baseball players in this book. *The Ballgame of Life* is about the kind of early training that makes some of the past and present major league players special for many more reasons than their statistics. The odds of any particular ten-year-old becoming a major leaguer are a million to one, but it doesn't mean that he or she can't learn the same lessons about integrity, the joy of competition, and the value of team relationships that great players learned when they were ten.

Peter Gammons
ESPN Baseball Analyst
Member, National Baseball Hall of Fame

Warmups

Introduction

Every player, coach, fan and parent at every level of baseball—from tee-ball to the big leagues—wants to be on the winning side anytime an umpire yells, "Play ball!" That's just human nature. Nothing in this book should be construed as attempting to diminish the competitive instinct.

Winning is not just a measure of success, however, it is the *result* of success. Winning comes from doing the right things in the right way, and this book is about skills that parents and coaches need in order to use baseball as a tool for instructing young baseball players how to win "the ballgame of life."

Especially in their early years, children need to learn lessons that baseball is uniquely designed to teach, such as patience, confidence, fairness, focus, good sportsmanship, and teamwork. This book is aimed at the parents and coaches who want to teach children those lessons but sometimes don't know how. We have proven exercises for you to do with your sons or daughters or the members of the teams you coach that will remind them—and you—that baseball is a *game* that is meant to be *fun*.

Between us, we have over seventy-five years in and around the game of baseball as players, coaches, agents, fans and parents. We love baseball, and we want kids to love it to. To do that, we need you parents and coaches to remember what you are trying to accomplish.

So let's play ball, with a heavy emphasis on the word *play*.

Dave Smith and Joey Aversa

Opening Pitch

The Starting Lineup

Before we begin, here is a lineup of proven practices to use when parenting or coaching young baseball players. These ideas underlie every single suggestion, story, piece of advice, and exercise found in *The Ballgame of Life*.

Leading Off: Make sure you take the time to teach the most important things first. Get your priorities straight: Teach integrity, respect, character, class, work ethic, friendship and personal responsibility. Baseball skills and drills should always take a back seat to these life lessons.

The Two Hole: Be honest and direct. Help your young players understand your thought process and purpose behind your instructions, advice and criticism. The candid way you deal with them will demonstrate the benefits of being truthful yet compassionate, even when it is not easy to do so.

The Three Hitter: Treat errors, mistakes, mishaps and failings as learning opportunities rather than as moments of shame, embarrassment or disappointment. Teach your young players how to turn negatives into positives and to keep everything in proper perspective. Show them you believe in them, especially when they are having doubts about themselves.

Batting Cleanup: Strive to be creative and enthusiastic in your approach. Remember that teaching young players to accept direction and criticism is 100% dependent on your ability to deliver it in a proper and constructive manner.

Hitting Fifth: Be open-minded and learn from others. When a coach or player or fan on your own or another team does something well or outstanding, acknowledge it, point it out to your athletes, learn from it, and show your appreciation by way of emulation.

The Six Spot: Guard against unrealistic expectations. This does not mean that you have to set the "expectation bar" low. It does mean that you should focus your energy, effort, time and talent on your young players' strengths, interests, and receptiveness to learn.

Batting Seventh: Set expectations and limits. All young players need (and really want) structure. This means there must be rules and they must be followed. However, be sure that the rules are not so rigid that they get in the way of having fun.

The Eight Hole: Be flexible and always have contingency plans at your disposal. Some days certain words or drills work, and other days they are a complete waste of time. Be prepared to switch to plans B, C, D, and/or Z when you are working with young players.

The Pitcher's Spot: Don't just tell them; show them! With young players your actions have a much greater impact on their learning process than your words do. So if you want them to become great adults, act like a great adult yourself—even when you might not feel like doing so.

Designated Hitter: Keep everyone involved. All players deserve a chance to play and learn. All parents have a right to be involved with their kids. All coaches should get a chance to coach. If you do this, you will have a real team.

The Goal of Every Great Coach and Parent

Let's start with us, not the kids. We are either the parents or the coaches—or sometimes both—of young baseball players who range in age from five to fourteen years old. (We'll leave the high school and beyond years to others perhaps more brave than we.)

Regardless of all of *our own* expectations, hopes and desires for our future Hall of Fame athletes, we all share at least one common goal, even if we occasionally lose track of it: We want our children to turn into happy and successful human beings with outstanding personal qualities. That, more than anything else, must be the primary goal of every baseball parent and coach.

Great parents and coaches don't create great athletes; they create great people. They do this by teaching children *respect:* respect for themselves; for their teammates and opponents; for umpires, coaches, parents, other adults; for the game of baseball itself. As Ryne Sandberg, the great second baseman for the Chicago Cubs, said at his induction ceremony to the Hall of Fame in 2005:

> I was taught you never, ever disrespect your opponent or your teammates or your organization or your manager and never, ever, your uniform. Make a great play, act like you've done it before. Get a big hit, look for the third base coach and get ready to run the bases. Hit a home run, put your head down, drop the bat, run around the bases. Because the name on the front is a lot more important than the name on the back. That's respect.

So our job as parents and coaches is to teach respect for a game that demands a good work ethic and high level of personal commitment and self-discipline in order to excel and succeed. We have to teach our children that playing fair and following the rules of the game is more important than the outcome of the game itself. How do we teach these things? By setting a personal example for them with our own outstanding personal conduct, by "keeping our back foot planted" in our own values and beliefs, by remembering that baseball is a game that is meant to be played.

Developing Life Skills to Win the Game of Life

For just a moment, let's take our minds off the baseball field and think about the real world and some of the challenges we adults face everyday:

- Getting up every morning and getting ready for work, even when we don't want to.
- Getting to where we are expected to be…on time.
- Interacting and communicating effectively with others.

- Performing tasks under time restraints or deadline pressures.
- Achieving personal goals and or quotas.
- Overcoming unforeseen difficulties and making necessary adjustments to overcome obstacles.
- Getting along with difficult, unreasonable, incompetent, unlikeable, or even dishonest people.

Now, here's the good news: Playing youth baseball gives every child the opportunity to learn and develop almost every single personal skill and quality needed to succeed in life. This is truly a remarkable and golden opportunity.

Here's even better news: As long as we adults don't "take our eye off the ball" and mess it all up for them, our kids get to learn all of those incredibly valuable life skills while laughing, smiling and playing with their friends the best game ever invented.

Think about how baseball does this:

- Baseball demands a *disciplined work ethic.*
- Baseball develops an *ability to cope with stress and pressure.*
- Baseball teaches how to *adapt and adjust to changing circumstances.*
- Baseball helps figure out methods to *meet and exceed expectations.*
- Baseball requires commitment to *complete our tasks and not give up,* even when we are tempted to do so.
- Baseball necessitates the *overcoming of setbacks, disappointments and injustices* by insisting on the *maintenance of pride, poise and composure.*
- Baseball encourages *respect and motivation* of teammates and colleagues.

A Formula for Success That Lasts a Lifetime

As coaches and parents of young baseball players, we have a ready-made formula for teaching our children how to be successful in life. The ingredients are right there in the game itself, and if our kids learn the lessons on the ball field, they will carry them over into the rest of their lives.

1. Commitment

Every successful baseball coach and/or parent must teach each little athlete the importance of making a commitment to play on a team. Baseball forces kids to understand they need to be at every practice and every game precisely *because* their teammates are counting on them to be there. It may be difficult to get this expectation across at first because children think (based on their experience up until now) that life is really all about them and their needs. Baseball, however, presents parents and coaches with an excellent opportunity to teach and reinforce the concept of making a commitment to others and living up to that commitment. If baseball accomplishes nothing more than this, it will be worth all the work you put into it.

A critical component of commitment is punctuality, and again baseball is great for teaching it. Games start on time, whether your child is there or not. If he or she doesn't want to bat last or sit on the bench, then best be on time. Learning the importance of being somewhere at a specified time is another valuable lesson that will serve your child well for life.

2. Listening and Learning

Baseball constantly reinforces the importance of listening and learning. Our young ballplayers are taught that first by their mom and dad, but it becomes even more obvious when taught by a coach (especially one who is *not* related). Learning to re-

A True Story

My dad was a stickler for being on time. He felt that it showed a lack of respect to whomever I was supposed to meet if I didn't care enough to be there when I said I would. As a parent he expected us to be on time, but as a coach he demanded it.

This was as clear as a picture of one of my fifth-grade teammates, Rodney. Dad as a coach would make us players run laps if we were late to practice, but when it came time to travel to other fields he never said what time to be there; he just said when the team would be leaving.

On the day of our team picture, Dad/Coach said we were leaving at 10:00 A.M. At the appointed time we left, all of us except Rodney. Rodney was late, and we didn't wait. Rodney barely made the team photo that year, but how he got in it is the best part. He wasn't in the front row with the rest of the short guys. He wasn't in the back row with the coaches either, but if you look real close, in the top left corner of the photo, you can make out the tiny features of a boy in a black and white jersey racing across the field, his baseball glove in hand.

I don't know what Rodney is doing now, but I do know he wasn't late again that season. He is also immortalized in my scrapbook as a personal reminder to always be on time.

spect authority, listen to authority, and comply with authority teaches kids that they have to meet and live up to the expectations of others—even strangers or people they don't necessarily know or even like. Every coach has rules, and learning why and how to comply with rules—even those that might seem silly or unreasonable—is another of life's valuable skills.

Baseball reminds little ones that not listening to the coach makes it harder for all their teammates to learn and become better players, since the coach has to stop and repeat everything again. Kids begin to understand that this is not only unfair but also unacceptable.

3. Winning and Losing Gracefully

Baseball offers one of the first opportunities in life to teach children how to win and lose gracefully. (Of course, a lot of parents and coaches never learn this lesson themselves.) But because it is a game with an obvious winner and loser, and because very, very few teams in baseball win every game they play, baseball offers the opportunity on a regular basis to lose gracefully as well as to be a good winner.

This is perhaps the skill that is most missing in modern sports and indeed in society in general. With younger children especially, there is the opportunity in baseball to demonstrate how to do this regularly. For example, most teams at this level shake hands after every game. It is important that the coaches and the parents support this ritual and insist that the kids take it seriously.

4. Play Hard, Practice Hard, and Have Fun

Baseball offers a great seven-word piece of advice to each child: *Play Hard, Practice Hard, and Have Fun.* This mantra begins building a work ethic in even the youngest child. All coaches and parents need do is create a supportive and enjoyable environment for kids to do their hard work. (And if we do it right, they won't even know it's hard work!) This environment gives children the confidence to attempt and achieve unfamiliar or uncomfortable tasks, face pressure situations, and meet or even exceed their own expectations. This new-found confidence can last a lifetime.

Virtually nothing we do as parents or coaches is more valuable to our young athletes than being a positive and upbeat role model while at the same time creating an enjoyable, supportive and secure environment for them to learn the game. The game of baseball itself will create an environment that allows our children to learn, develop and refine (through both success and failure) a good strong work ethic and sense of confidence in their ability to achieve. All we need to keep in mind is that they are learning a lot more from our actions and reactions than they are from our words!

TEACH YOUR PLAYERS THIS

Always show
respect for your elders,
your teammates,
your opponents,
your coaches,
the umpire,
yourself and
the game.

Life Skills Learning Drill 1

"Learning the Game Together"

The goal of this drill is to teach children how to assimilate knowledge about the game. But more importantly it allows you to spend time and bond with your child and teach him or her that love is more important than any game—even baseball!

Remember the great scene near the end of the movie *Field of Dreams* when Kevin Costner's character gets together with his deceased father to "have a catch"? Baseball is a game that was invented to let parents and children, grandparents and grandchildren all bond like no other game. Don't ever jeopardize the beauty of this by being so focused on trying to turn your son or daughter into a professional baseball player. If kids are destined to make it to the big leagues, they will get there anyway. So put your relationship ahead of your personal goals and enjoy the beauty of the game together. You can teach children a game that they can enjoy as a player and/or spectator for the rest of their life. Take your time and do it right. Explain what makes the game so great. Tell them why you enjoy it so much. (Explaining "why" is just as important as explaining "how.") Tell your young athletes what it is you are going to teach and why it is you are doing a particular drill and how it can make them better ballplayers. Learning baseball is truly an excellent opportunity to spend quality time together (the operative word is *together*). So the drill is to play catch, or take a few swings, or field a few grounders, but to do so in a way that you explain what you are doing and why and allow yourself time to just be with your child.

Life Skills Learning Drill 2

"Hit the Dirt Drill"

The purpose of this drill is to relax, cut loose and get dirty. Baseball's a game; it's supposed to be fun. So is life!

Gather your team together in the dugout. Look them all over closely. Then announce that they are just way too clean to be a good team. Tell them to drop their gloves and take the field. Slide, dive, roll, and do whatever you have to do out there for the next five minutes to get those uniforms dirty. The more mud, dirt and grass stains, the better. The laundry person (Mom?) may not like this drill, but the kids are going to love it.

Life Skills Learning Drill 3

"Team Routines That Bind, Bond and Work"

The goal is to teach kids the importance of routines. Show them how complying with routines lays a good foundation for becoming successful—at baseball and at life.

Kids, like adults, find comfort in routines, and comfort is the key to getting kids to start opening up, relaxing, and having fun. Team routines also have a bonding effect. One of your team routines could be that the batting order for the game is based on who shows up on time for batting practice. (Remember: If you are fifteen minutes early for practice, then you're late!) Another routine might be using the same fielding drill before each game. Or you can have the team come up with a phrase or statement that you all shout between innings, such as: "One, two, three, let's get some runs!" Routines like this are easy to make up and kids love them.

Second Inning

Your Limited Window of Opportunity

First, the bad news: There will come a day when your little super star will determine that he has learned about as much about baseball (and about life) from you as he or she can. Your instructions, advice and demonstrations just won't resonate like they once did. When this happens, don't feel bad. It's as natural as Tony Gwynn's swing.

Now here's the good news: We parents have our kids' attention at the most critical and instrumental point in their life. If that limited window happens to be just the first five years of life, take it. If that window happens to stay open for another eight, nine or ten years, it's even better. Those early years are the most important time in any person's life in terms of formation of personality, self-image, confidence and values. We get the first shot at setting the stage for our little ones to have a positive and healthy appetite for learning, competing, and developing personal skills that will last a lifetime. This is a big responsibility, but there is no one better suited, more vested, or more motivated than a child's parent to successfully tackle that responsibility.

And if we decide to coach young children—our own and those of others or just those of others—we have a very similar window of opportunity. Let's face it, few of us are going to coach high school baseball, much less college or professional ball. So for better or worse, it is the five- to fourteen-year-olds that we will coach, from tee-ball until they head off to high school. We cannot treat our players as if they are adults. They are, by definition, kids. We have no alternative but to treat them as kids, which means that the life lessons we teach them are much more important than any baseball skills we may (or may not) have to impart.

Some Things to Always Remember

Whether we are "just" parents or parent-coaches or "just" coaches, we have to remember whom we are dealing with. We are dealing with children who want to have fun, who want (to a greater or lesser degree, depending on the individual boy or girl) to learn the great game of baseball, and who more than anything else are looking to the adults in their lives—*especially* their parents, teachers and coaches—to show them how adults are supposed to act. So here are a few things to always remember as we try to keep our priorities straight in teaching young children about baseball:

1. We are their everlasting role model.

Do you realize how great this is? Ask yourself this question: What are the most important qualities I hope my children or players ultimately develop in their lifetime? If you are like most parents and coaches, the list will include most if not all of the following traits: confident, happy, optimistic, positive, team player, pleasant disposition, hard working, popular, easygoing, kind, understanding, generous, courageous, etc. Okay, now what? Remember that we have our kids' attention at the most impressionable and formative time of their lives. Our actions, conduct and words will literally serve as their personal blueprints for the kind of person they will someday become. This is extremely powerful and extremely important.

During this limited window of opportunity, it will be *our* words, *our* actions, and *our* deeds that have the most significant impact on our children's likelihood of developing those wonderful traits we just identified. Better us than some selfish, trash-talking, hot headed, spoiled, overpaid celebrity or professional athlete!

2. We are a walking, talking "instructional video" for our children.

You want your child or player to approach life with a positive attitude? Then act as if things are fine. You want your child or player to be optimistic? Then believe that most things will turn out well. You want your child or player to be kind to others? Then be kind to your own child or the child next to him or her. You want your child or player to be confident? Then have faith that your team will get better. You want your child or player to be a good sport? Then demonstrate good sportsmanship on the ball field—both from the stands and from the dugout.

You get the picture: Even if these qualities are not necessarily natural to you and your disposition, you owe it to your child or player to consistently demonstrate them anyway. Anything less would be a disservice to a youngster. Never assume that a child will learn those desired qualities later in life from someone else. The task is yours and yours alone. You hold the blueprints. If you use your limited window of opportunity correctly, every person your child encounters in his or her lifetime will be grateful to you, even though they won't necessarily give you the credit.

33

A True Story

Here is an excerpt from an actual essay one twelve-year-old boy wrote for his eighth grade class:

The person who inspired me that I chose to write about is my baseball coach. Coach has had a substantial impact on me by teaching me baseball skills and good sportsmanship; he has fostered good relationships with other players and their families, he has taught me good leadership skills, and been instrumental in building self-esteem and motivation. During the past four seasons that he has coached my baseball team, his coaching has led us to three winning seasons (two of which we won championships) and one losing season. During the middle of our losing season, he gave us a strong motivational speech that inspired my team to win the rest of our games for the remainder of the season. I believe that he is a wonderful teacher and mentor and a strong inspiration to me and many of my teammates.

Coach has impacted my life in a positive way. He has focused on building my athletic skills. He has taught me the rules of baseball, the fundamentals of the game, the importance of having the right attitude, and the proper mechanics of the game. He has taught me specific skills associated with developing one's swing and one's pitching motion.

But I am most grateful for the emphasis and importance Coach has placed on teaching us about teamwork. He felt that it was more important for us to value working together as a team than on our individual successes. In this capacity, he fostered positive and strong relationship between players. There are many times through this process that I know Coach was frustrated with us because he thought we weren't valuing this important message, but we did, and we know that we will be better for it.

Last year when I had some trouble, Coach helped me through it and encouraged me to disregard negative comments. His wife shared with my parents that Coach was aware that I was under a great deal of stress, and he discussed with me several ways to alleviate this stress and improve my game.

As one of the oldest players on my team, I was appointed one of the leaders by the Coach. I was expected to show leadership, be responsible, help the players that weren't so good, and be a positive influence on the younger players. Sometimes I know that I didn't do as well as Coach expected, but he didn't lose faith in me. He always turned a negative situation into a positive one. When we had a horrible season this year, Coach kept a positive attitude. He didn't care if we won; he just wanted the players to have fun.

Coach has been a positive influence who has fostered self-esteem when I needed it the most. For these reasons, he has been a big inspiration in my life and someone I feel you should know.

3. Children need positive reinforcement, not critical advice.

The world of most children is already full of people telling them what they cannot do and say—all day, every day. The last thing they need or want is another critic when they are trying to have fun playing a game with their friends. When it comes to youth baseball, stow the criticism and lay on the praise.

You might say, "But my son doesn't pay attention" or "My daughter can't seem to step and throw correctly" or "That one kid on my team drives me crazy." Calm down. Youth baseball is not the end of the world. Yes, some kids are better ballplayers than others. And yes, we do have a responsibility to teach the kids the game. But there are ways to teach and correct constructively and with good humor that will go a long way towards teaching your little Babe Ruths how to play and respect the game. In fact, we are going to teach you a lot of them in this book.

To Coach or Not to Coach?

Here is one of the big questions in youth baseball: Should you coach your own son or daughter? The answer is not as obvious as it might seem. Certainly, we need good coaches at every level of the game. You may well be one of them. And those of us who have been around for a while know that one of the reasons to coach your own kid is to prevent him or her from being coached by one of the really bad coaches who sometimes volunteer in youth baseball leagues.

However, it is important that coaches ascertain their true agenda for coaching their own child or children. If you feel that you were cheated out of your own major league career and want your progeny to make up for it, or if you are thinking how nice that championship team trophy will look on your desk at the office, save your child the misery and let someone else coach the team. Perhaps you can be an assistant coach or a team mom or dad or keep the scorebook or chase after foul balls. The truth is that a lot of kids don't even *want* their own parent to coach them.

If you have a healthy relationship with your child, and if you truly *like* working with children (you'd be amazed how many coaches really *don't*), and if you have a basic understanding of baseball appropriate to the age group you want to coach, then by all means volunteer. If you are asked to coach, you will have a great time and develop a special relationship with your own son or daughter and many other players.

If you don't have kids of your own or want to continue coaching after your own kids are grown, do so. Some of the best coaches are those who do *not* coach their own children. But again, be careful of your motives. If you like the power that coaches have over kids or hope someday to land that professional coaching job or just like winning for its own sake, then think about doing something else with your spare time. If you love the game of baseball and want to teach it to young people (along with some basic life lessons), then find yourself a team or a league that could use someone just like you.

TEACH YOUR PLAYERS THIS

Always tell the truth. You must do this even when telling the truth is difficult or embarrassing.

Life Skills Learning Drill 4

"Midgets vs. Giants"

The goal of this drill is to demonstrate that hustle and hard work can pay off. It also breaks the stereotype that equates size with athletic ability.

Divide your team into two: the tallest guys on one team ("The Midgets"); and the smallest guys on the other team ("The Giants"). You pitch for both teams. Each player gets one hit, no matter how good or bad it is. Use an "over the line" format where base running is not necessary, only hitting and fielding. After each three outs, announce "Hustle in; hustle out" and then begin pitching as soon as the first batter gets in the box. Finish practice with this drill and they will leave smiling and be looking forward to the next practice.

Life Skills Learning Drill 5

"All or Nothing"

The point of this drill is to practice getting comfortable with pressure situations (with others counting on you) before you actually face them in games. Counting on others to succeed is also useful in real life.

Occasionally stop your practice and ask who feels confident enough to bet the coach a "team lap" around the field. Someone will volunteer. If the player is an infielder he or she goes to short and you hit a ground ball. The player has to cleanly field that ground ball and make a good throw to first base. If he or she does, you take a quick lap around the field. If not, the whole team runs the lap. For outfielders it's a fly ball that has to be caught with a good throw to second base. The whole team is counting on the player, and they love it when you have to run. If they have to do the lap, they give the player a good-natured ribbing. You can make up all types of scenarios using base runners and different game situations, and you can use different incentives for success and failure. Be creative and make it fun.

Life Skills Learning Drill 6

"Four Corners"

This drill is designed to teach teamwork, accuracy and conditioning. It is also teaches that there are consequences for mistakes and failure to concentrate—in a game as well as in life.

Divide your team into several four-cornered squares. Have the players throw the ball around the square (always throwing to the left). If someone drops the ball or throws it over someone's head, that player sits down and that team is down to three. You keep tossing the ball around until only one team has two or more players left in its square. You can also use this as a conditioning drill. As soon as a player throws the ball to the left, he or she takes off running to that same corner where the ball was just thrown. The goal is for everyone to make it around the square to all four corners without a bad throw or dropped ball.

The Main Jobs of Parents and Coaches

If you decide not to coach, it doesn't mean your opportunity—or your responsibility—to help with your child's development of life skills through baseball is over. Every coach has a few players whose parents basically view their kid's involvement in baseball as "free babysitting," and there is absolutely nothing that drives a coach crazy more than this. The coach is not supposed to pick your son or daughter up for practice or drive him or her home afterward. It is not up to the coach to call to remind you that there is a practice or game the next day and that Junior or Sissy should be on time with complete uniform and equipment. The coach is not supposed to discipline or punish your child for outrageous and unacceptable behavior on the ball field. And please, do not expect the coach to teach your little ones basic moral values that are not taught at home, or the perils of drugs or riding a bike without a helmet, or the facts of life. These are, and will always be, your jobs.

How Parents Who Don't Coach Can Help

Even if you cannot or don't want to coach, don't leave the entire task of teaching your child about baseball (or life) to the coach. First of all, you will be missing too much. Especially at a younger age, the basic skills of baseball are ones that virtually anyone can teach. Throwing and catching, running the bases, swinging a bat, and hitting a ball—these are all so basic that you can certainly do them with your son or daughter. The rewards are great in terms of your relationship with your own child if you assist in his or her early baseball training.

Besides, every coach of young children will tell you that the best players are those whose parents practice with them regularly. Baseball is a sport that requires lots of "reps" (repetitions). There is a lot of emphasis on hand-eye coordination and taking swings and fielding grounders or fly balls. You can do this with your child, and even if you have no baseball ability at all you can get a spouse or sibling or aunt or uncle to help out, while you shag balls or give encouragement from the sidelines.

As your children grow older, you can continue to be involved in their baseball development, even if you can no longer keep up with their skills. For example, you can become an assistant coach or team mom or dad or just the greatest fan in the world. You can take photos or bring treats or take the team out for ice cream or pizza. You can help the coach by organizing a phone tree to notify the team of last-minute changes or keeping the scorebook or getting sponsors. At the end of the year, you can be the parent who remembers to take up a collection and get the coaches a card and a gift to thank them for all the good work they have done with the team.

Let us say a word about being a parent-fan. The first thing you need to realize is that kids hate it when their parents embarrass them. This is so obvious that it should go without saying, except that so many parents don't seem to "get it." It's one thing to cheer little Johnny or Joanie along with the rest of the team, but it is quite another thing to make a big deal when he or she is at bat or makes a play and then ignore the rest of the team. What's worse are the parents who think that it is their job to coach their child from the stands or to criticize the coach or the umpires from there. And then there are the parents who decide that it is helpful for them to belittle their own children when they fail or to ridicule or ride players or coaches from the other team. Believe us when we tell you that your son or daughter will resent you for it and will walk away from baseball at the first opportunity you allow.

Remember: You are teaching your child a life lesson every time you cheer or jeer, every time you show them how mature adults should act or act like a jerk yourself. You have only yourself to blame or credit, either way. The coach may give you some direction either verbally or by example, but it is primarily up to you what kind of a parent you are going to be on the ball field.

How Coaches Can Lead

Okay, you're the coach of young baseball players. You've got their "semi-undivided attention." Why? Because you're *The Coach!* When it comes to young players, this simply means: "You've got the stage because my mom and dad told me to listen to you. So entertain me for the next hour and a half." Never will it be more important to know your audience than now. You may want to talk to them about being able to tell the difference between a fastball and changeup when it leaves the pitcher's hand, but they may still be struggling with just being able to tell a ball from a strike regardless of what speed it's coming at them. Be flexible in your approach to coaching based on your players' personalities and ability to concentrate. Otherwise you run the risk of losing them early on. Here are a few tips that might help:

1. Always leave them wanting more.

Your players should leave your practices anxious and excited to come back to the next one. The greatest words a coach will ever hear is, "Is practice over already?" The trick is to know when to stop coaching (because you have just about lost their "semi-undivided attention") and to start having fun. Keep in mind, the attention spans of kids at every age are just about half as long as adults think they should be and only about an eighth as long as you wish they were. Don't be discouraged if you didn't get to "teach" for a full hour and half. If you do it right, they will learn just as much in the "having fun" part of practice as they did while listening to your expert advice and participating in your well-thought-out technique drills!

2. Always demonstrate good character.

You can virtually assure yourself of being a successful coach by teaching young people good personal values, strong ethics, and fine moral qualities. If you do, no one will even remember (or care about) your lifetime won-lost record. Teach kids to do the right things even when no one is looking, no one cares, or no one expects it. You do this primarily by doing the right things in front of them when no one is looking, no one cares, or no one expects it. For example, if you want to teach them patience, then don't lose your temper. If you want to teach them that all kids have value, then don't spend all your time with the best players. If you want to teach them that baseball is fun, then have fun yourself. More than anything else, never let the scoreboard or game situation cause you to lose sight of your primary objectives and true reasons for coaching.

A True Story

My little boy just turned five and is starting his first season of tee-ball next week. He's been excited about this since the first time we drove by a little league field together (about three years ago) and he saw little guys wearing uniforms. He wanted to get right in the middle of that.

He had his first team meeting with his new coach this week, where he got his first jersey ever and found out he was playing (by the luck of the draw) for the Padres. He was so excited he literally shrieked with joy. He couldn't stop holding and staring at his new replica San Diego Padre uniform, and he definitely couldn't stop smiling. He took it to bed with him that night and insisted on wearing it to school the next day. There he had seven more hours to process how significant this really was.

When I picked him up at school that afternoon, he informed me that we had to give Uncle Joey a call right now and "tell him the good news." Joey, of course, is a coach with the (real) San Diego Padres. I dialed the number for him. When Joey answered the phone, my son announced with glee, "Hey, Uncle Joey, guess what? I'm going to be playing for the Padres too! I'm number 7. What number are you going to be?"

For a brief moment both Joey and I got to witness a little boy experience (at least in his own mind) the thrill, joy and excitement of making a big league baseball team. No matter what else happens this year, it's already been a good season.

3. Separate your expectations from theirs.

We can almost read your mind: You're thinking that, with the way your best player (or your own child) is already hitting and throwing, if you just get him or her the right coaching, some private lessons, regular trips to the batting cages, the proper encouragement and direction.... Stop right now! Ask yourself, "Whose game, whose life, is it anyway?" Right now is the perfect time for you to start separating your expectations from that of your players, because if you don't you may be depriving them of some of the best times they will ever have during childhood. If you have them so focused on making all-star teams or getting ready to play high school ball, they may completely miss the pure enjoyment of the game. They may overlook how great it is just wearing a uniform and getting it dirty. They may never know the satisfaction of breaking-in a new glove. And for certain they will miss all the little things that make the game of baseball so wonderful: the great smell of a freshly cut field, the crack of a bat, the sounds of cheering from the fans, or laughter on the bench. They might miss all this because their coach or their parents have focused them on achieving expectations that are really not theirs.

TEACH YOUR PLAYERS THIS

Always maintain your pride and poise. A poor loser or a person with a bad temper is not a true winner.

Life Skills Learning Drill 7

"The Bat Toss"

This drill demonstrates that there are many new, unusual, creative and fun approaches to improving baseball skills and techniques. This idea of "thinking outside the box" or "trying something you never thought of" is important in every aspect of life.

Hitting the ball well at any level requires that you "throw your hands at the ball." Have one player at a time go over to one of the foul lines so nobody can get hurt. Draw a line straight through the middle of the field and put a marker about twenty-five yards out. Now have each player take a full swing with good mechanics and release the bat so that it lands in the middle of the field near the marker. This will cause them to take a natural and fundamentally sound swing. Players love competing with each other and themselves and it's one of the few times in baseball where you can toss the bat without getting yelled at or tossed out of the game.

Life Skills Learning Drill 8

"Smile Practice"

The purpose of this drill is to teach players not to be afraid to show they are having a good time. When the kids grow up, they will need to know how to "keep smiling."

Every so often, even in the middle of whatever you're doing with them, stop and ask the team to come over and show you their smiles. Surprisingly, some kids are actually afraid to smile. Sometimes they avoid it out of embarrassment or fear that whatever they just did well was a fluke and won't happen again. Either way, your job is to make sure they smile and enjoy their success—whatever it is and whenever it occurs. Occasionally, just call them over and tell them it's "smile practice." Joke with them. Ask them to tell you something funny. Tell them something funny. Ask them to show you their "home run smile." Nothing will help create a more positive association between baseball and life skills than smiling. Make it a team habit.

Life Skills Learning Drill 9

"Ask, Don't Tell"

The idea of this drill is to get the players invested in their own development. They will certainly have to do this in high school and beyond.

Never assume you know what your troops want to learn or need to know. Ask them what they want to learn. What do they need to work on the most? What are they most worried about when it comes to playing games? This approach allows you to identify their immediate weaknesses and concerns, minimize them, and ultimately turn them into strengths. You end up building their confidence based on their priorities, at their pace and not yours. At first, this may seem like too much of an individualized approach. But if just one of your players is willing to share his or her weakness and concerns, rest assured that the other kids have almost the same ones in one form or another. By taking this approach, you will not be leaving any of the players behind. More importantly, by teaching things that help them overcome the very things that are most important to them, you give yourself a decent chance of keeping their "semi-undivided attention."

Fourth Inning

Success (and Failure) Leads to Success

Whether you are a coach or parent or a coach/parent, read this next sentence carefully: *It is our job as adults to create scenarios and opportunities in which our young athletes can achieve and experience success.* On the field, at the park, or even out in the backyard, we must set up situations where what the kids do is right. We have to find their strong suits.

For example, if children just starting out in baseball are natural at throwing a ball, great. Have them throw balls as long as it remains fun. If they are better at hitting, have them hit till the cows come home. If they run like the wind, then by all means have them run their little tails off. As kids get older, keep promoting the positive. The ones who can pitch, let them pitch. The ones who can catch a fly ball, put them in the outfield. If they can steal home, teach them how to steal home.

Whatever skill they gravitate towards is your opportunity to create multiple successes. The reward for multiple successes at an early age is the mental confidence gained from doing something that draws praise and accolades from adults.

On the other hand, don't ignore the value of failure in achieving success. This sounds like an oxymoron, but it is true. First of all, kids are going to fail at baseball. In fact, baseball is designed for failure. Nobody gets a hit every time, no pitcher has a 0.00 ERA, no one never makes an error.

But the failures in baseball can lead to success—both on and off the field—pretty directly, if we let them. And it is the job of parents and coaches to make sure that this happens with young players. We have to make sure that success leads to success and failure leads to success.

Little Successes Lead to Big Successes

For young children, every success they experience—no matter how small or insignificant—is wonderful. Why? Because young people don't yet have a gauge for measuring how important an accomplishment really is. Isn't this great? Wouldn't it be wonderful for adults if everything were equal—doing the dishes and signing the big deal, going to a movie and having a wedding, hitting a nice drive on the golf course and helping to save the world?

Every accomplishment is a big one to kids. That's why—crazy as it seems—we give them trophies for just showing up in tee-ball. Baseball makes young baseball players smile and feel good, and it is human nature to keep doing things that make us feel good about ourselves. They may just start out with the objective of hitting the garage door with the ball, but in no time they will be focusing on hitting a specific square on that same garage door...with velocity! Little successes naturally lead to bigger ones in baseball.

Positive reinforcement and praise are beautiful music to children's ears. Not only do they enjoy hearing it, they take it to heart. Since they don't yet have a "real world gauge" in which to measure their accomplishments and improvements, *they need us to do it for them.* Don't wait for your little superstar to get his or her first hit in a game to celebrate. Celebrate the little things that might normally go unnoticed. For example, celebrate the fact that he or she tried out a new batting stance or played a new position, for it shows a willingness to overcome fear and try new things. Celebrate the fact that a child concentrated on something for longer than fifteen minutes in an effort to accomplish it or improve, for this is a first step in creating a work ethic. The upside to giving praise to our kids is that we are giving positive reinforcement to each and every one of their incremental steps in their effort to become not only good baseball players but also good human beings. What's the downside to giving such praise? There is no downside!

"I am so proud of you" is a magical phrase for kids, but most parents and coaches don't use it nearly enough. Maybe it's because we are too focused on results and not on effort, on winning rather than playing the game, on the college scholarship instead of a great set of childhood memories. Let's be honest here, our little leaguers are out there on that field because we want them to be there. They didn't call around and find out when baseball signups were, and they certainly didn't empty their piggy banks for the enrollment fee. You wanted them to have the experience of playing ball, and at least in part they are accommodating *your needs and desires.* That alone should make you very proud, and you should tell them so after every practice and game. If they go all season without a hit, they still went to the plate and faced their fears. If they miss a ground ball and take it in the chin, they still got in front of it. Is there anything that they could do that is more deserving of your pride? The point here is simple: There are a million different reasons to

A True Story

We were the only team in the league that had girls playing. In our small town there were not enough third-grade boys to field a team. There weren't enough girls for an all-girls team either, but the only people who really cared were a few of the coaches on teams we played against.

We played "coach pitch," meaning that each coach pitched to his own team. If the kid didn't hit the ball in three pitches, a tee was brought out and the kid hit off of it. It was a very introductory league. In fact, we weren't even supposed to keep score. It seemed, however, that some well meaning parent always kept an unofficial scorebook, just to let their kids know (unofficially) if they had succeeded or failed.

Our team improved every practice, not only in baseball skills but in paying attention and sportsmanship as well. However, one of our players had not had a lot of success, baseball wise at least. Sarah was a great kid and tried really hard, but she had never played before and never really got the hang of catching a ball that was thrown or hit to her.

Our last game of the season we played a team that "unofficially" had won all of their games. The coach of the other team yelled and screamed at his kids—the classic taskmaster coach. I am sure he meant well, and from personal knowledge I know him to be a nice man, but the message he resorted to at that last game was, "Boys, you're getting beat by a team that has girls on it."

With two outs in the final inning, with runners on second and third, our team was "unofficially" leading by a run. One of the players on the other team hit a long fly ball to left field. In the movies this is where everyone moves in slow motion, mouths open, yelling in silence, and the crowd all rises to get a better view of the flight of the ball. All alone in left field stood Sarah. She never moved a step. She never looked up into the sky. She simply raised her arm in the air. SMACK, the ball had finally found Sarah's glove!

That Sarah caught the ball didn't really amaze me—miracles happen in baseball every day. What was so special was how our players reacted. Every player on the team sprinted to left field and literally carried Sarah and her smiling face off the field.

tell your young ballplayer, "I am very proud of you." Quite frankly, you don't even need a reason.

Failure Is a Critical Component of Success
One of the most difficult things in the world for us parents and coaches to accept is that our children's failures (no matter how big or small) are critically important—and in fact necessary—for them to ultimately achieve success of any kind. Failure or adversity gives children an excellent opportunity to do several positive things:
- Learn how to cope with disappointment.
- Analyze what they did wrong.
- Seek instruction on how to do it correctly.

But without a doubt the best part of failure is that it is the result of our children actually trying to accomplish something. Someone once said, "People don't fail; they give up." And any failure is better than never having tried at all. So every failure is yet another good opportunity to teach our children the importance of "giving it a try," trying your hardest," and "never giving up." For example, when Babe Ruth (arguably the greatest hitter of all time) was hitting his record-smashing home runs, he was also setting records for most strikeouts in a season. Every single one of the Babe's strikeouts was an important part of one of the greatest individual achievements in the history of baseball. Why? Because every time the Babe went to the plate he was trying his hardest to hit the ball out of the park. Sometimes he did and sometimes he didn't. That's baseball: You take the good with the bad. Life is the same way; and baseball prepares our children for that reality.

As our children get older, of course, we will naturally broaden and define the definition of "not trying" to properly elevate their horizons. For example, we will tell them that "not trying" means not hustling or not listening to the coach or not giving the proper encouragement and support to teammates when they are struggling. The key for parents and coaches is to properly ascertain when they are ready to take on new duties, responsibilities or expectations.

Controlling Our Reaction to Their Disappointment

Rest assured that our children will naturally feel disappointment when they don't meet their own expectations (whatever they are). Some kids will actually walk back to the bench crying after striking out or skip treats and head for the car immediately after losing. All kids will look to Coach or Mom or Dad for a reaction to gauge just how extreme their display of disappointment should be.

Here are our options:

- *Positive Reaction:* "Good effort; you took some nice swings; you'll get them next time."
- *Negative Reaction:* "You've got to stay focused; never take a called third strike; that pitch was out of the strike zone."
- *Overreaction:* "That was horrible; you let your team down; if you don't care, you shouldn't be on the team."

Every season, at nearly every game across the country, you will hear negative reactions and overreactions by parents and coaches alike. It's painful to listen to. Kids will get over their own disappointments in baseball, but they may not get over ours!

When things go bad for our favorite player (and sometimes they will a lot), the positive reaction is appropriate about 99.9% of the time, especially the younger the child is. A negative reaction or even an overreaction may very well be the first thing that comes to our mind, especially if we think we are just trying to help our young ballplayer improve his or her skills. But the fact is that the criticism will do no good at that point. All that can happen is that the child will feel worse about himself or herself. Whatever learning needs to take place will happen later, long after the game is forgotten. Our job in this situation is to show our children how to gracefully overcome adversity with class, dignity, pride and poise. If we want to give our children one personal quality that will set them apart and above in today's crazy world, this is it.

TEACH YOUR PLAYERS THIS

Never complain, whine, point fingers or blame others when things go wrong. Just work harder!

Life Skills Learning Drill 10

"The World Series Hero"

This drill teaches preparation for pressure situations while at the same time instilling confidence in children that they will be able to perform in those situations.

Create a baseball scenario and then let your player achieve it. For example, put a ball on a tee. Announce that the score is tied, it's the bottom of the last inning, the bases are loaded, there are two outs, and the count is full. Now let the batter take swings until he or she gets the game-winning hit. No matter how long it takes, the child still gets the feeling of success. There is no limit to the different scenarios you can create, and when the kids ultimately face similar situations in a real game they will either consciously or subconsciously remember that they have been there and succeeded before.

Life Skills Learning Drill 11

"The Happy Ending"

The goal of this drill is to teach children to always finish strong and to stay with something until they accomplish it.

Always end on something positive and then make a big deal about it. If you are taking batting practice, always end it on a line drive hit. If you are taking ground balls always finish with a good play and strong throw. If you are working on pitching, the last pitch should be a strike. As time goes by, you will find that finishing on a positive note will mean that at least subconsciously the entire session was a success.

Life Skills Learning Drill 12

"That Ball's Outta Here"

This drill gives children success immediately and then incrementally. It also challenges them to improve and stay enthusiastic while doing it.

Take your child and the batting tee out to the centerfield fence. Set the tee just far enough away from the fence that when he or she makes good contact the ball will clear the fence. Use a tennis ball if you have to. After the first one goes over, celebrate it like it was a major league home run. Each session will allow you to move the tee back just a little farther.

Fifth Inning

Developing a Healthy Definition of Winning

During every baseball season, several tragic stories spring up—all with the same pathetic theme: Some mom, dad or coach gets so caught up in wanting his or her child to be victorious in a game that he or she engages in some embarrassing, socially unacceptable, or even criminal act. These stories of adult failure (that is, failure to be adult) are so sad, shocking or disturbing that we decided not to include them in this book. There's no sense depressing ourselves. Besides, you've already heard them, read about them, or even observed them yourself.

Anyway, the people who are that nutty about baseball—and life, and raising kids—won't read this book anyway. But you are, so let's talk about you. The first thing to admit is that you like to win. We all do. You don't have to be a genius to figure out that winning is more fun than losing. And if our kids are going to play baseball beyond the first year or two of tee-ball, then they are going to have to develop a healthy attitude about winning (and losing). That attitude must begin with you—their parent and/or coach.

The next thing to admit is that we all get carried away sometimes. That's part of the fun of games, including baseball. What White Sox fan didn't go crazy when Paul Konerko hit that grand slam in the second game of the World Series when his team was down 4-2? What parent or coach doesn't look like Steve Martin in the movie *Parenting* when his son finally made a game-winning catch in right field?

And we can be disappointed as well: A bang-bang play doesn't go our way: The ump makes a terrible call that changes the outcome of a game; the best player on our team strikes out at a key moment. Or even worse, the coach on the other team or one of the parents in the stands is a real jerk. Maybe he or she even yells something really stupid—maybe even at our child or at his or her own. Worse case scenario, we see someone actually cheating: *Cheating in a kids' game! What kind of person cheats in a kids' game? Why, it's enough to make your blood boil! Why, no one should be allowed to get away with that! Why, I'm not going to put up with it any longer! Somebody's got to do something! If you won't handle this, I sure will!*

See how easy it is to get caught up in it? See how easy it is to forget that we are the adults and that this is only a game? So the emotions are real, and there is no sense denying or ignoring them. But still, there are at least twenty or thirty pairs of eyes on us at every ballgame that are fixed on each and every adult on the field—and especially on their own parents and coaches. They are the eyes of our children, and they are watching us to determine not only what is acceptable behavior but also how they are to judge this question of winning and losing.

Keep Winning in the Proper Perspective

If you haven't already done so, you need to change your whole attitude about "bad calls," "bad umpires," "bad coaches," "bad plays," "bad decisions," "bad losses." Why? Because none of these "bad" things are truly "bad." In fact, they're actually "good."

They are all "good" because they are real, concrete, non-life-threatening opportunities for your child to learn some very valuable lessons about life. Former college football and baseball coach Ad Rutschman taught that there are times in every game (and in life) when things do not go well—in fact, they go really badly. He also taught that during those times it is our *pride and poise* that allow us to overcome adversity. Think about it: Who goes through life without adversity? Who doesn't lose a job or a friend or an election, go through a divorce or a bankruptcy or a financial setback, suffer a defeat, make a mistake, regret a decision? How are we supposed to prepare ourselves to handle these situations? Baseball, yes, baseball, can help. Early on, adversity, frustration and defeat on the ball field can provide our little ones with an excellent opportunity to develop their own personal pride and poise. And just as Coach Rutschman predicted, these two qualities will serve them well for a lifetime.

As adults, we all know that life is not always fair, right or just. We know that things don't always go the way we want them to. We have learned that we will not always be successful in everything we attempt. We have also discovered that some people don't play by the rules, have poor judgment, make bad decisions, and do things that disappoint us. We call this the ballgame of life, and we recognize that it can be beautiful whether we win or lose. What matters, literally, is how we play the game.

Kids, of course, do not know this yet. It is not obvious or instinctive. They think, "Maybe winning is all that matters; maybe we are judged (and judge ourselves) solely by whether we win or lose." After all, they see this all the time on television: The world is divided into winners and losers—on game shows, real-

A True Story

When I was born, my father put a baseball in my crib. From that time on I cannot remember a day when I was not intrigued by every aspect of the game. However, at age eight, when I was finally allowed to put on a uniform and start my baseball career, I was bombarded with verbal hurdles from coaches and teammates. They went like this: "You're too small;" "You can't hit;" "You're too slow;" "Soccer might be a better sport for you."

However, I loved the game of baseball too much and refused to accept these things as insurmountable hurdles. Instead, I took them personally, as if they were challenges.

Then the silent insults started. I was always chosen last to hit in practice, and when I played I always hit last in the order. People who doubted my abilities grew in numbers. My desire to prove them all wrong also grew. At twelve years old it reached a pinnacle. I put so much pressure on myself to prove that I could be a good hitter that I would actually come back to the dugout in tears every time I made an out. I put so much pressure on myself that I couldn't even be coached. My failure at the plate was all consuming in my mind and nothing else (tips, advice, coaching) even registered in my head. This game that I thought was so great and that I loved so much was tearing me apart.

I had always dreamed of making a little league all-star team, but that dream would never be realized. Little league baseball had become my personal nightmare. I never got a hit that entire year. I was zero for the entire season! My only solace was that I could field. My glove became my salvation. It would not betray me and I gave it all my attention. I convinced myself that as long as I could field, I could play. So I kept going.

Two things happened the next year that saved my baseball career. First, Dad convinced me that last season was behind me and I needed to focus on the upcoming season. He was not only convincing, he was inspiring and remained my biggest fan. He never doubted me or my abilities. He kept me focused on the positive parts of my game and was determined to turn a bad situation into a good one. After watching me go through the personal anguish of that previous season, he made a point of instilling his own laid-back, confident demeanor in me. I developed a new personal motto that went: "I can because I'm gonna and I will." I even wrote that motto on the bill of my cap.

The second thing that happened that year was that I got on a new team with a new coach who emphasized just going out and having fun on the field. My dad continued to put things in the proper perspective for me by making sure I understood that baseball was a game and that games are supposed to be fun. I was finally able to relax and enjoy myself on a baseball field. I thrived. The hits started falling.

Did this experience change things for me? Considering that I just finished my fifteenth year in professional baseball, I would have to say that it changed everything. To this day, the only thing I tell my own two boys is to go out, play hard, and have fun...it works!

ity shows, drama shows, comedy shows, even religious shows. And most of all they see this in sports: The winners are praised, honored, rewarded, celebrated; the losers slink off into obscurity.

It is up to us to teach them that "you win some, and you lose some," and that both are okay. Sometimes we are on the winning side; often we are not. This is the very nature of baseball, and it is also the very nature of life. So if we teach our children that when we win it is great, then we have to teach them that when we lose we will be fine and there is usually something to learn.

By observing your good example of pride and poise in the stands or the coach's box, children will learn to take minor setbacks in stride, graciously forgive the human errors of others, and overcome them without having a meltdown. If, on the other hand, you want children (and eventually young adults) who react to setbacks by hollering, screaming, making excuses, blaming others, sulking over things that don't go their way, reacting out of anger, and losing all control of their emotions, then just keep setting that example for them. We guarantee you'll get your wish.

Start with a Healthy Definition of Winning

If your definition of winning is confined to coming out on the favorable end of a final score, you are actually cheating kids. First of all, nobody wins all the time—especially in baseball. You know that the higher you go in baseball, the more parity there is. By the time players get to the major leagues, teams are so even that the best team in baseball usually wins less than six out of every ten games, and the worst teams win four out of every ten. So, maybe your team wins every game in tee-ball. (That probably means that the teams or the coaches were not equal to begin with.) Maybe your team wins in coach-pitch. (Perhaps your coach can pitch to little kids better than other coaches.) But by the time they get into kids-pitch and certainly if they go on to play on travel teams or in high school, young ballplayers have to learn how to accept defeat gracefully.

Solely focusing on the final score of a game belittles and causes kids to miss some very significant accomplishments:

- They practiced hard to get ready for that game *(building their work ethic)*;
- They got their uniform on and got to the game on time *(building a sense of responsibility and commitment to self and teammates)*;
- They got on a field in front of a crowd and put themselves in a new and maybe uncomfortable situation *(learning to face fears and building courage)*;
- Maybe they even got a hit, made a catch, stole a base in the course of the "loss" *(accomplishing a personal achievement and experiencing success)*;
- Unless the parents or coaches ruined it, they played a wonderful game with friends where they most likely laughed, cheered and encouraged each other *(building a sense of teamwork and camaraderie)*;
- They shook hands with or cheered the other team at the end of game *(developing a sense of good sportsmanship, fair play, and respect for others)*;
- They might have had treats after the game or gone out for ice cream, pizza or a burger with some of their teammates *(having fun, laughing and bonding with friends)*.

If they accomplished half of these things, tell us again how important that final score was. Winning is not just simply a matter of keeping score. A "win" or a "loss" only becomes so when you define it as such. Sure, nobody likes to lose. Nothing in this book is suggesting that you encourage it. But winning or losing at the level of young ballplayers has a far broader definition and context than the final score of a game.

Children only really lose when the adults they look up to lose that perspective. The minute you start measuring success by batting average, earned run average, or won-lost record you just let the scoreboard beat your child—and what a tragedy that is.

TEACH YOUR PLAYERS THIS

Avoid vulgar
language and
bad behavior.
It cheapens your
character and
causes others to
think less
of you.

Life Skills Learning Drill 13

"The No-Shoe Sliding Drill"

This drill is designed to make children laugh, bond and relax while learning a difficult skill.

Sliding into a base is a somewhat difficult skill to teach and learn. Part of the reason is that kids are afraid of turning an ankle or hurting themselves on the dirt—especially if it is hard or has stones in it. So take them out to the outfield and have them learn to slide barefoot on some nice soft grass into a temporary home plate. This reduces the chances of getting injured and also teaches them to keep their feet in the air as they slide. Teach the feet-first slide, because that is the one they should use most of the time. Save the head-first slide until they are older, because that slide is easier to get hurt on. When you move into the infield, again start by sliding into home and then move to the other bases. You can also put out a number of large plastic trash bags in front of a base and have them slide onto the trash bags until they have gotten the motion down. These drills are fun and make learning to slide easier on them and on you.

Life Skills Learning Drill 14

"Dive to Survive"

The purpose of this drill is to teach kids to go all out and give it everything they've got on every play. It is also good practice for learning to perform under pressure. Plus, it's fun to dive in the grass!

Again, go to the outfield grass first, so the kids are more willing to dive. Line all the players up and have each one take turns diving to knock down a line drive or a grounder. Start by throwing the balls softly and gradually increase the speed as they succeed in knocking the balls down. Eventually, use the bat to hit the balls. Throw or hit the balls either to the player's left or right randomly. All he or she has to do is knock the ball down so it doesn't go past. If the player gets to the ball, he or she "survives" and goes back to the end of the line. If the ball gets past, he or she is out of the game. Keep playing until there is only one survivor. Then move into the infield and use the drill in each of the four infield positions so they get a feel for knocking the ball down at the different positions. (Don't worry about catching the ball or throwing it for now. That will come later.)

Life Skills Learning Drill 15

"The Team Cheer"

This drill builds team spirit and both focuses and loosens up kids.

Every team has to have one cheer. Start using it in practice and then carry it over into the game. Use it at the beginning and end of a practice and game and also between innings or when you are changing a drill. Keep it extremely simple and involve the players as much as possible. For example, one favorite cheer is to have all the players huddle up and put their fists together in the center. Then one of the players yells as loud as possible, "One, two, three," and the rest of the players scream, "Go, Yankees," or whatever the team name is. One hint is for the coach to pick a different player each time to yell the "one, two, three." This could be somebody who made a good play in the field or, conversely, somebody that the team needs to "pick up" because of an error or a strikeout. Make sure that every player gets a chance to lead the cheer over a period of time.

Sixth Inning

Finishing What You Start

There are two reactions that we parents and coaches cannot accept from young ballplayers: "I can't" and "I quit." We cannot accept them because they are worse than any swear words our most foul-mouthed player can come up with. In fact, they are poisonous to our self-respect and sense of self-worth.

This is because our young charges will never accomplish anything in life if we allow them to develop these attitudes. "I can't" allows kids to not even try. "I quit" is even worse, because it has the addictive effect of allowing a person to get out of doing something once they find out it is difficult. And life is difficult, in case you haven't noticed.

Fortunately, baseball is a great proving ground for children to learn that something they thought was impossible—hitting a ball, catching it, throwing it to the right base, tagging someone out, sliding into home, running from first to third on a single, bunting, pitching a strike—can be done and can be done by them. And baseball also teaches that if you try long enough and don't give up, there is a place for you in the game. You might not play second base for the Houston Astros or the Los Angeles Angels of Anaheim, but if you stick with baseball and don't quit, you can play for your high school team or in a park league. Or when you grow up you can sit in the stands and keep score, or teach your own kids about the game you love, or even coach or help coach a team of young players.

But if children are allowed to say they "can't" or they "quit" in baseball, the second time will be even easier, and the third time even easier than the first two. And if they decide they "can't" or they "quit" in baseball, what's to say that they "can't" or they "quit" in school, a job, a marriage, or parenting? Accordingly, it's very important to jump on those phrases early and effectively if you are a coach or parent of a young ballplayer.

Now, this does not mean that you are allowed to force-feed children your own love of baseball. There is probably nothing sadder than the kid who is out on the field trying to live out his mother's or his father's or his coach's dreams. There are plenty of other sports or activities that children can pursue that are equally good and may even be better suited to their skills or temperament, and when they figure those out, you'd best be there to support them—even if you can't stand tennis or chess or badminton or whatever it is they choose. But if and when children exhibit interest in exploring baseball, even in a very tentative way, it is important that we not let them say they can't play the game or want to quit trying. Sure, they can stop playing baseball—at the end of the season, if they still want to. But once they've started, it's up to you, the adult, to teach them that they have to finish what they start and they can't let down others to whom they have made a commitment.

Figure Out What They Really Mean and
Then React Appropriately

The first couple of times that children throw down a bat or a glove and announce "I can't do this" or "I quit," it's most likely an attempt to draw a reaction from you. The odds are also good that you are going to hear those two phrases back to back: "I can't do this," followed by "I quit!"

Here's our first advice: *Don't overreact.* In fact, this is usually a good time for no reaction at all. Kids get frustrated learning baseball. It's not an easy set of skills to develop, and they often want to take it out on somebody else or get some sympathy. What you do next is critical. Calmly remind your little charges that you understand their frustration. Remind them of all those times they thought they couldn't do something but finally succeeded (e.g., tying shoelaces, climbing to the top of the jungle gym, riding a bike). Tell them this is just another one of those times and that you will help them until they finally succeed. The key then is to help them succeed. After a child who is struggling finally successfully accomplishes a task (whatever it is he or she has been trying to do), end the session. If it is catching a ball, keep making soft tosses until one hits the mitt and sticks in. If the kid can't hit a pitched ball, go back to the tee until he or she does. Then stop. If it is pitching, quit as soon as one of those pitches goes over the plate. The important thing here is to avoid making a potentially bad situation into an actually bad situation. If you handle it right, it will turn out to be one of the most positive sessions children have ever had, because they will have achieved three very important things:

- Proved to themselves that they actually "can" do it and that the phrase "I can't" was totally untrue;
- Learned that if they had actually quit (as they had threatened to do) they never would have achieved success;

A True Story

Ned joined my son's team in fifth grade. He was the tallest, most athletic-looking kid on the team. His first appearance at the plate in every game forced fielders to back up and coaches to start shifting their players into positions for what would most likely be a hard hit long ball. But Ned was in fact the most uncoordinated boy on the team. Game after game he struck out in each at-bat, hardly ever making contact with the ball at all. Opponents got to know him and learned to pretty much ignore any threat they once felt from him. Parents from the competing team no longer let out loud "oohs" of fear when they saw Ned approach the plate. We faithful followers, however, continued to encourage Ned with each at-bat: "This one's yours, Ned. You can do it."

Over the next four years of watching one another's sons make progress with their fielding, pitching and hitting skills, we parents from the various schools in the area all pretty well came to know which boys were capable of what. We remained competitors, urging our own boys on to victory as loudly as we could, but something gradually changed through the years. It showed up in small ways. When one of the players committed an especially embarrassing error, no matter which team the boy was on, both sides of the field would join the chorus of "That's okay, just shake it off." When a boy got up limping after sliding into base, we'd ask about him after the game, even if he was on the other team. To me, the most obvious change was when Ned came up to bat, struck out, and went back to the bench. After a while, the competing parents no longer cheered for their team's good fortune. I wondered if it was because they now considered him no threat or if this was just another example of the "softer, gentler" competitors into whom we all had evolved.

Our coach was a patient, encouraging guy who made sure every boy played no matter what. So of course Ned came up to bat at least once in every game. Then one game in the eighth grade, when the season was almost over, Ned came to the plate. We parents started our usual banter of "This one's yours, Ned. You can do it." To everyone's astonishment, Ned's bat connected with the first pitch. Whack! Just like in the movies, that ball flew way over the outfielder's head, who was playing in, of course, because it was only Ned up there. Ned took off running and we parents went wild, cheering him around each base until he actually made it all the way home. Unbelievable! Ned had his first hit ever and it was a home run.

We couldn't stop cheering, but gradually I realized that the rousing cheers for Ned were not all coming from our side of the field. The parents of the boys on the other team—who had all watched Ned struggle for four years, who admired his determination, who must have been silently rooting for him to get at least one hit in his young life—were all standing and yelling, "Way to go, Ned! We knew you could do it!"

- Found that using the two pathetic phrases "I can't" and "I quit" didn't draw the intended reaction, so there is probably no sense in using them again—at least not with you.

Teaching the Importance of Finishing What We Start

Baseball is a team sport. This is another thing that is great about it. Because it is a team sport, it allows us to teach our children about commitment and accountability to others. For once they sign up for a team, the team counts on them—not only to show up but to try hard and practice and get better. Playing on a team is an awesome responsibility: Quitting or not trying (for any reason) is not an option. If a kid learns no other lesson from baseball than that one, it has done its job.

There might be times during the season when children will get tired of baseball, be upset with their coach or teammates, or won't feel like going to practice or a game, but there is no quitting in baseball. There are usually only eleven or twelve players on most teams, so if one of them doesn't show—especially for no good reason—then it makes it harder for the other players. Even if your child is no Joe DiMaggio, he or she can still fill the spot and chase down a ball hit to the outfield or draw a walk and score the game-winning run.

Still, some children do give up, and at some point in the season you may have to remind them of your little pre-season agreement: Even if they beg and plead (in tears) with you to let them quit, and the season to this point has been a nightmare for both you and them, you must stay firm on your goal of teaching the importance of completing whatever it is we start—no matter how difficult. If you have to, tell them that if they still feel the same way about it next season they don't have to play, but for now they are committed to finish a full season and they will! This may be one of the most difficult things you will ever have to do as a parent or coach, and it may even break your heart. Just keep in mind, however, that if you let your young ballplayers quit once (for any reason) you are not doing them a favor. Instead, you have set a precedent for them to quit again and again and again in their lives. The importance of honoring commitments is the very least that baseball can teach our kids, and that lesson will pay dividends for years to come.

Finally, here is a sad reality: It is often adults—parents and especially coaches—who give up on certain kids, not the other way around. We have all seen the young player who is stuck in right field, always bats last, only plays the minimum number of innings required by league rules. That is not the person who is giving up. It is usually an adult who has given up on him or her. It is an adult who has said "I can't teach this child" or "I quit trying to teach this child." The reason adults do this to young children is very sad: They want to win at youth baseball so badly that they forget about some of the very youth who need them the most. It is these adults who do not finish what they start, and the kids can see this too.

TEACH YOUR PLAYERS THIS

Never use the
phrases "I cant"
or "I quit." These
phrases are poisonous
and must be avoided
at all cost.

Life Skills Learning Drill 16

"An Encouraging Word"

*This drill gets young players thinking about conse-
quences for using negative or discouraging words. It
breaks bad habits early and teaches them to put the
team and their teammates ahead of their own frustrations, outbursts, or use of bad language.*

Be aggressive regarding certain words or phrases you don't
want your players to use. Tell the players that using them is completely unacceptable because they hurt the team. Tell them that
same list applies to you as well and that using these words and
phrases (even accidentally) will result in a team lap around the
field (which you will join). After the team finishes the lap, every-
body has to huddle around and say something positive or encouraging to the violator.

Life Skills Learning Drill 17

"See the Ball, Hit the Ball"

*The purpose of this drill is to focus on the things that
players can control and give themselves every chance
to succeed.*

The reality of the game of baseball is that kids get quickly
overwhelmed when they start thinking too much. The time to
analyze and worry is definitely not when they are playing.
That's when they need to keep their mind clear and react to the

ball. Otherwise they will be beat before they even step onto the field or into the batter's box. During batting practice, have them try not to think about anything but "seeing the ball" and then "hitting the ball." This will also teach them to go with the ball where it is pitched. Then, when they are in a game, especially if they are in a slump, simply yell to them, "See the ball, hit the ball!"

Life Skills Learning Drill 18

"Phantom Ball"

This drill teaches focus, visualization, and proper mechanics. It also offers positive reinforcement to struggling players and teaches everyone to laugh, relax and have fun.

Rarely do you come across a drill that is hysterically fun and totally effective, but the "Phantom Ball" drill is one of them. Your team takes the field for infield and outfield practice. Use the exact same routine you would do before every game. Except in this practice you don't take a ball onto the field. Take a bat and pretend to hit a fly ball to the left fielder and yell "second base." The left fielder pretends to catch it (with good mechanics) and pretends to make the perfect throw to the cutoff man, who also happens to be in the proper spot to cut off the throw and then pretends to throw it to the second baseman. The second baseman pretends to tag the phantom runner and then make a perfect throw to the third baseman, who pretends to catch it, tag another phantom runner, and then make the perfect throw back to the catcher. The catcher pretends to catch the ball, takes it out of the glove, and hand it back to the coach. This routine goes on for a full infield-outfield session. If you do it right, your team should not make a single error the whole session—at least in Phantom Ball!

Seventh Inning

Team, Teammates, Teamwork

Baseball may be the ultimate team sport. First of all, you need a minimum of nine players to play the game correctly, and that is before players start specializing in pitching and catching. Second, players have to be able to play both offense and defense. Third, no one player can completely dominate a game. Every hitter makes outs, every fielder makes errors, every pitcher gives up hits and runs.

So baseball is a wonderful venue for teaching our children one of life's greatest concepts: teamwork. *Teamwork* is defined by *Webster's New World Dictionary* as "joint action by a group of people, in which individual interests are subordinated to group unity and efficiency and coordinated effort, such as an athletic team." If your son or daughter, or the players on the team you are coaching, can learn teamwork, it will serve them well throughout their lives in work, family and community relationships. Being on a team satisfies children's (and adults') strong need to "successfully belong."

The first step in team is just showing up. Children commit to play all season long because their teammates are counting on them, and they soon learn this is a two-way street when they are left short-handed or when one of the better players on the team goes on vacation or just blows off a game. As the season goes on, they start appreciating the fact that their teammates are all living up to their obligations to one another. Having the same cool uniform and cap with their team name blazoned across their chest adds to the special feeling that they have become a part of something bigger than just themselves.

Belonging to a team gives kids the opportunity to be part of something greater than themselves. Accordingly, learning to work together as a team allows children to experience and understand that bigger goals and bigger accomplishments are possible when done with others. Besides, it's always more fun to celebrate winning and commiserate about losing with teammates than it is to do it alone. The concept of team may be the real beauty of youth sports: kids together overcoming setbacks, celebrating joys, and discovering the meaning of true friendship.

What Children Get from the Team

Legendary college football coach Lou Holtz would tell his players, "Once you learn to work with people you can accomplish anything." Tackling adversity is always easier when done in numbers. Having teammates offers children the opportunity to overcome their fears and anxieties together ("safety in numbers"). It provides them a larger sense of courage, strength and confidence to overcome things collectively that they might normally back away from individually. This is the true beauty of teamwork. When these larger tasks are achieved together, special feelings start to form in children: loyalty, trust, respect and cooperation. They learn that the best way to do something does not always have to be their way. They learn that it is important to have others count on them, and conversely for them to count on others. They begin to establish a newfound sense of confidence in themselves because of their teammates. Deep and lasting friendships often follow.

Learning the teamwork necessary to play baseball promotes a sense of purpose like nothing most kids have ever experienced before. They learn that sacrifices made for the good of the team is a new, unique and special way of showing consideration, value and respect for others. Another tangible benefit is the learned ability to work with others to achieve something that they could have never achieved on their own. In some respects they will find this humbling. But that serves to open the door to mutual esteem, respect and admiration for teammates. The end result: a special feeling of camaraderie that is not matched anywhere else.

Although it is a popular sports cliché that there is no "I" in "team," the truth is that on every team there needs to be at least one "I" and sometimes more. Every team needs one or two players who quietly tell themselves: "I will practice and play really hard so that my teammates will practice and play harder too." It needs one or two players who say, "I will be there to encourage my teammates when they get down or when things don't go well for them." It needs one or two players who say, "I will do whatever I have to do to help my team, even if it means playing positions I don't like to play or sitting on the bench for an inning or two so they can play in the game." It is these "I" players who make their teams good and their teammates better. It's no coincidence that "inspirational" starts with "I." Don't hesitate to teach this quality to children.

A True Story

One of my good buddies in high school, Jimmy D, didn't look like a baseball player. He didn't run, hit or field as well as most of the guys on any of the youth baseball teams he played on growing up. Heck, he didn't even look that great in a baseball uniform. So the odds were not very good that he would ever be able to make our high school varsity baseball team. He didn't make it his sophomore year or his junior year. Now here it was his senior year, his last chance, and he was once again gearing up for tryouts and the almost certain disappointment that was to follow. The tryouts came and went, and as expected Jimmy's name was missing from the published roster. His baseball career had officially come to an end.

Jimmy was disappointed but not necessarily surprised that he didn't make the team. After all, our school had a good baseball team with a lot of great athletes. Several of those kids went on to play college baseball, a couple of them went on to play professional baseball, and one guy, Todd Christensen, went on to be an All-Pro tight end with the NFL Oakland Raiders and was even given a baseball tryout by the Oakland A's. By all honest assessments, Jimmy just wasn't in that league. Nonetheless, it couldn't have been easy for the coach to cut Jimmy, because not only was he an upbeat, enthusiastic kid, but he also loved the game of baseball and it showed. Jimmy studied the game, talked the game, knew all the nuances of the game—from giving signs to keeping an accurate scorebook.

Even after Jimmy was cut, he would swing by the baseball field after school and watch practice. He would shout encouragement from the bleachers and even chase down an errant foul ball hit into the stands or parking lot. I think he did it just because he liked throwing the baseball back onto the field.

A few weeks into the season, one of the players on the squad was suspended for excessive public partying with another team's cheerleader at a school dance the night before a game. It was a dumb move by a player who had hit .487 his junior year and had a good shot at a college baseball scholarship with even a halfway decent senior season. But team rules were team rules, and this kid was definitely in violation of those rules and was out for the year.

The following morning, Jimmy D was asked to report to the coach's office in the athletic department. When Jimmy walked through the door, the coach tossed him a varsity baseball uniform with the number 18 on it. Jimmy had just made the varsity team.

Now, Jimmy did not play much. I'm not even sure he got a hit all year. He spent most of that season keeping score, tabulating statistics, and coaching first base. He threw batting practice, shagged balls, and got to play just enough to earn a varsity letter. He immediately bought himself a new letterman's jacket and wore it proudly.

I loved seeing Jimmy D in that jacket and the great big smile that always accompanied him whenever he wore it. Ironically, I always felt like I was a special part of that great success story, because I was the kid that wore uniform number 18 the first few weeks of the season...right up until that fateful dance with the cheerleader!

Teams Are Made Up of Stars and Role Players

The fact is that from almost the very beginning of their baseball career, children are either one of the stars of the team or a role-player. Both are needed. Both are important. And both make up the complete team. The stars are the ones who are picked first in the draft, chosen for all-star teams, join traveling squads, and eventually play for their high school and perhaps college teams. Only a minuscule number of the stars ever get to play professional ball, and an even smaller number make it to the major leagues. Role players are those who can play a particular defensive position, lay down a bunt or get a key single, steal a base or throw out a runner, pitch an inning or two when the starter falters.

Everyone has some degree of God-given talent. For a very few, their major talent lies in playing the game of baseball. Even at a very young age, you will know whether a certain child "has it" or not. Whether or not that talent is developed depends largely on the child, although parents and coaches can either nurture it or destroy it. But even if a child is not going to make a career out of baseball, he or she can contribute to the team.

A good work ethic, strong desire, and sense of commitment are what lets one child excel and another fail. There is no denying that good genetics and athletic ability go hand in hand. However, many of the most "genetically blessed" people in the world never develop good athletic skills. Some of the greatest natural athletes in the world today are buying tickets and sitting in the stands of games as spectators watching less blessed athletes play the game for big salaries. Genetics are important, but they take a back seat to desire and hard work. Those qualities are the "great equalizers" to size, strength and speed. Remember Mark Twain's great line: "It's not the size of the dog in the fight; it's the size of the fight in the dog!" Time after time in baseball, that statement proves to be true.

With the exception of speed and size, you can improve on almost everything else in baseball with hard work, good technique, and a strong desire to keep getting better. We need to teach our kids to focus on those things they can control and ignore the rest. The trick is to make this challenge enjoyable for them. You have to convince them that the best feeling in life is working harder than others and succeeding with the talent you have. Creating such strong desire, work ethic, and appetite to compete will serve children in every facet of life, long after they have retired their mitts and cleats to storage.

TEACH YOUR PLAYERS THIS

Work hard
without being told
to do so. That is the
difference between
personal success and
personal failure.

Life Skills Learning Drill 19

"Team Motto"

This drill teaches how to build team spirit right from the beginning. It also gives kids permission to relax and be silly, even when playing baseball.

At the end of the very first practice give the team an assignment. Tell them you want them to spend time thinking and talking about what they want their team motto to be for the season. It doesn't matter how crazy, goofy, serious or funny it is, *just as long as they pick it and they like it.* After they come up with it, start and end every practice and game by huddling up and putting your hands together, saying the team motto aloud, and then breaking (like a football huddle).

Life Skills Learning Drill 20

"Nicknames"

This drill is a natural for building team spirit. It also teaches your players how adults can relate to them in a playful yet respectful way. You may even give a kid a nickname for life, so choose carefully!

Over the course of the season, give each of your players a nickname. Try to give them one that reflects their strengths or outstanding qualities or a key play that they make. For example, if someone makes a great catch in the outfield, you can use the nickname "Wheels" or "Clutch" or anything of a positive nature.

That way, whenever you refer to that player, it will instantly have a positive connotation, even when you are pointing out something he or she did wrong or needs to work on.

Life Skills Learning Drill 21

"Pizza Time"

The purpose of this drill is to learn how to build team spirit. But a second lesson to be learned is how to have fun in a public place while still maintaining a sense of order and respect.

Find a good pizza parlor and use the heck out of it during the season. "Pizza time" can even become a team chant anytime a player does something exceptional. The team will do a lot of bonding there. You want to celebrate the accomplishment of team goals, individual goals, or maybe even just a great play or unexpected clutch hit. Everyone can chip in for pizza after the game, except maybe the player who had the winning hit. This is also a great place to involve some of the other parents, not only in chaperoning and helping to pay for the pizza but also in developing a sense of community among themselves.

Eighth Inning

Know Your Players, Not Just Their Names

One of the biggest mistakes both parents and coaches of young ballplayers make is rigidity: You learned a certain way, they must learn the same way; this worked with other kids, it must work with this group of kids. Forget it! Each child is different, and each group of children is different. So pay attention to those who are in front of you and adapt your parenting and coaching to them.

Kids come in all personality types, just like adults do. There are the really aggressive ones, the shy or hesitant ones, the slow learners and the naturals. What's more, they interact with one another. The aggressive ones will overwhelm the passive ones, especially if the other kids are in the minority. The slow learners will frustrate those who "get it" right away. Your job is to balance the needs of the various personalities and make sure that none of them get lost in the shuffle.

If it is your own child we are talking about, you may need to take the coach aside and explain how your son or daughter reacts to things. For example, if a child hates to be yelled at, the coach should know that. This doesn't mean that the coach won't yell, but at least he or she might be a little more sensitive. On the other hand, little Johnnie or Joanie is going to have to learn to deal with a variety of people in life. It might start with parents and teachers and coaches, but eventually it will include bosses and neighbors and spouses and even children of his or her own. So part of your job as parent is to teach your child that adults have different ways of acting—just like friends do—and that part of growing up is learning how to deal with them.

If you are a coach, your job is multiplied by eleven or twelve. You simply cannot treat each kid on your team the same. Some might be going through really tough times at school or at home, and you may not even know about them, except that you know something is wrong. While you are not a counselor or social worker, you may well find one of your players reaching out to you for help. Be ready to respond, even if it is only to help the child find the help he or she needs. Many a coach has experienced becoming a very important figure in one of their player's lives, long after the kid has stopped playing baseball.

For the most part, however, coaching is learning how to best deal with a group of kids, both as individuals and a team. Sometimes kids need a symbolic kick in the tail, other times they need a pat on the back. Sometimes they need a cheerleader who can convince them that they can win, sometimes they need a philosopher who tells them it's only a game. Being a coach of young baseball players is an awesome privilege and responsibility. Remember: No one will ever remember what your won-lost record was. What they will remember is whether you taught your players the life lessons they needed to learn.

Coaching the Aggressive Personality Type

So you've got a little daredevil who goes full speed, headfirst into everything and has absolutely no fear of anything. Congratulations and condolences are both in order. The aggressive personality type offers parents and coaches some interesting challenges and opportunities.

Now we all know that being "willing and able" is the perfect combination for achieving success not only in sports but also in just about all other facets of life. The good news is that this kind of player is willing to accept almost any challenge and probably won't even wait for you to present it. In those cases, your task is to monitor and prioritize those challenges to make sure that the child is able to take them on successfully at the proper age. Every coach talks about players who are willing to run through a brick wall in order to win, but you really don't want children running through too many brick walls to win a game of tee-ball. The bad news is that your little one is literally willing to give it a try. You have to make sure he or she doesn't...at least not without wearing a helmet anyway!

The risk you run with aggressive-personality-type kids is that if they are allowed to try and run before they can walk, they will naturally fall flat on their face, potentially lose interest, and move on quickly to the next challenge. Once again, failure is a critical component of success in baseball, and the aggressive personality type will generally not be overly discouraged by the experience. However, we still need to help them avoid the major failures or traumatic setbacks that aggressive personality types are more prone to expose themselves to. We need to consistently praise the effort and courage that these kids exhibit but still keep them focused on the fundamentals necessary to achieve their goals. If we can show them how to walk first, then running will be all that much more fun when they finally do it.

A True Story

When I was coaching in our house league for boys ten and eleven, the very first practice I would take them out to the third-base bag and tell them that we were going to learn how to steal home. (They hadn't been allowed to do that in our league up until then.) We spent the entire practice on it.

Stealing home is a lot of fun. At that level, it is mostly a matter of getting a good lead, watching for a passed ball or a wild pitch, and then exploding toward home plate and sliding in safely. All the kids loved doing it: the good players and the weak players, the aggressive ones and the shy ones, the experienced players and the neophytes. If they were ready and did it right, there was almost no chance of getting caught, because the pitcher and the catcher had to make a perfect play. And whether the runner was safe or out, it was a fun play, with lots of excitement and cheering from the fans and a big call by the umpire.

I made it a team goal that every player would steal home at least once during the year. Of course the more aggressive players did it in the first couple of games, but then even the more timid ones starting trying it. On each pitch they would break from third toward the plate to a line I had drawn about a third of the way down the base path. If the catcher missed the ball, the kids would just keep going and try to score. If the catcher caught the ball, the player would put on the brakes and scramble back to third. I never criticized a player who made an out. Instead the whole team would give him pats on the back for trying. Most of the time, the runner was safe and our team had another run.

By the end of the year, every player on our team had stolen home successfully at least once. We became known as "the team that tries to steal home every time." This gave us an identity and a sense of camaraderie and made every player on the team feel that he had made a contribution to our success that year.

In the championship game, however, one of our kids got caught wandering too far off third and was picked off, but the entire team and our fans gave him a big round of applause anyway. We ended up losing the game by one run, but I doubt that any of our players remember the final score. I'll bet every one of them remembers stealing home that year, however.

The energy and enthusiasm of aggressive personality types needs to be properly channeled. To make the most of all of their natural desire, we need to give them a "mental checklist routine" that allows them to use up some of that extra energy. If we can get these kids going through a checklist of fundamentals, mechanics and goals while preparing for a practice or game, the combination of those aggressive mental skills with their already aggressive physical skills will make them twice the player they already are. Coaches often refer to this as "controlled aggression." The goal is to get kids to play "within themselves." Once his or her mental checklist becomes ingrained, look out!

Finally, aggressive personality types are often natural leaders. Peers follow them on the playground just to see what they are going to do next and watch them on the sports fields with admiration for their courage and daring. Accordingly, for everyone's sake, our ability to teach such players good leadership skills on the ball field is important. This effort on our part will be rewarded in ways we cannot yet imagine. A good leader makes a very valuable member of any team at every age, regardless of how well he or she ultimately swings a bat or throws a ball.

Coaching the Shy or Hesitant Kids

Every coach has heard or said this about certain players: "He just doesn't have that same fire and burning desire I had" or "She's just a little hesitant to get out there and get right in the middle of it like I did when I was a kid." Well, maybe these kids are just a little smarter than we were at that same age. Shyness or hesitancy is generally a result of being a bit more cerebral than physical, and there really is nothing wrong with this. Caution is a natural survival skill, whether it is in fielding or hitting or pitching a ball, or in interpersonal relationships. It gives kids a chance to stop, look, listen and learn. After having a chance to do things, analyze them for a while, and then get comfortable with the whole idea, most shy or hesitant kids are fine.

Some young athletes just need more time than others before they are comfortable dealing with a hard ball being pitched, hit or thrown from just a few yards away. What some call "shy" or "afraid" or "passive," others call "smart." The fact that children understand that there is some risk involved in playing baseball (or in living life) is not necessarily a bad thing. After they have gotten comfortable with the idea that there are various ways to avoid being hurt, they will gladly jump into the fray. We can help them by being sure to respectfully acknowledge those concerns (no matter what they are) and then talk and work through them.

For example, at least initially some kids are more comfortable talking about hitting a fastball than actually doing it. That's okay. It gives us an open door to do some fact finding about what is preventing them from just grabbing a bat and jumping into the batter's box. In this scenario, they will most likely tell you that they don't really like the idea of getting hit by a hard baseball. What they are really waiting to hear from us is "I don't blame you. Nobody does. Even the big leaguers don't like getting hit by the baseball. And if they do get hit (and it doesn't happen very often), it hurts for a little bit, like when you fall off your bike, and then in a few minutes you're fine. Plus, I can teach you how to turn to get out of the way so at least the ball will hit your back and not your face." This type of answer does four important things:

- It gives proper and respectful *acknowledgment* to a very real concern or caution.
- It gives *assurance* that the child is not the only one who is afraid to get hit by a baseball.
- It gives an estimated *comparison* of the type of pain that might be experienced and how long it will last.
- It gives *comfort* that there might be a way to avoid or minimize the pain by learning the proper technique.

Thus, we have *acknowledged, assured, compared* and *comforted*. Now that "cerebral mind" of the shy child has everything it needs to analyze and overcome his or her cautions and concerns.

Once they have had the opportunity to analyze and overcome initial concerns and cautions at least mentally, children will be ready to physically face those fears. The trick here, however, is to *let kids choose the forum for physically facing their fears.* If they want to start out in batting cages and hit hard balls at high speed with little chance of being hit, great. If they just want you to throw wiffle balls or tennis balls to them in the backyard, that's fine too. Positive reinforcement is in tall order here. Applaud their swings, get excited about their hits, and heap on the praise. Learning to face our fears (in any capacity) is deserving of celebration. Our little players' confidence level will continue to climb and they will start challenging themselves...but at their pace and not ours. Even if their advances are not as rapid or as substantial as we would like, relax. It's only a game.

TEACH YOUR PLAYERS THIS

Always look people directly in the eye when you are talking to them. Good eye contact shows respect and sincerity.

Life Skills Learning Drill 22

"Mental Routines"

This drill tries to help players create a mental routine that requires concentration, focus, and mental discipline. These are all skills needed later in life.

Teach older players which are "hitter's counts" (1-0, 2-0, 2-1, 3-0, 3-1) and which are "pitcher's counts" (0-1, 0-2, 1-2, 2-2, 3-2). During batting practice, call out a count and ask the player whether it is a pitcher's count or a hitter's count. Then pitch the ball. If the player swings at a bad pitch on a hitter's count or doesn't swing at a good pitch on a pitcher's count, then point that out. Then during a game, you can call out to a batter: "hitter's count" or "pitcher's count" as a way of focusing. Another example for younger players: When you hit ground balls, have the fielders count the number of hops between when it left the bat until it hit their glove. Also you can mark a different color on each ball you use for infield practice. After a player has fielded the ball and made the throw, ask him: "What color was on that ball?"

Life Skills Learning Drill 23

"Checking the Checklist"

The goal of this drill is to help players focus on the mental part of the game by teaching them how to go through a mental checklist. This improves their visualization skills and sense of self-discipline.

Help players create a simple three-step approach to hitting that they will visualize as they step into the batter's box:

Step 1: Get my feet right (good hitting stance).

Step 2: Hide my hands from the pitcher (hands up and behind my head with the bat in the proper starting position).

Step 3: Try to find the ball from the second it leaves the pitcher's hand (then hit it hard, right in the middle of the ball).

Life Skills Learning Drill 24

"Balls and Strikes"

This drill is specifically designed to let the more reserved personality types physically face their fears and develop a comfort level. They will need this skill in life.

Have the players stand one at a time in the batter's box with a helmet but without a bat. (They can even have their glove on if they want.) Throw slow pitches to a catcher and have the "batters" shout out whether it's a ball or strike as it crosses the plate. This forces them to go with their gut reaction and be physical (instead of cerebral) in the process. They will be so focused on whether the pitch is a ball or strike that they won't realize they are overcoming their fear of being hit by a pitched ball.

Ninth Inning

Final At-Bats for Parents and Coaches

First let's summarize the good news: Young children are easy to teach. Learning is what they do most of the time. They expect it. They are used to it. They are ready for it. Also, baseball is a great vehicle to use to teach some very important life lessons to youngsters.

Now the bad news: Young children are learning, even when we don't realize it or don't want them to. They are watching us as coaches and parents, not only when we are trying to teach them something about baseball but *all the time.* So if we aren't careful, we'll be teaching them the wrong lessons and not even know it.

For example, it is amazing how many coaches and parents think it is a good idea to have a beer after (or even before or during) a youth baseball game. What we are communicating when we do this is that drinking is somehow connected to baseball. A few years from now, these kids will be teenagers and we will be trying to convince them that they do not need to drink to have a good time, but all they will remember is that Coach So-and-So ordered a pitcher of beer every time the team went out for pizza, and all the parents joined in. So the logic goes something like this: baseball = fun; baseball = beer; therefore, fun = beer.

The same could be said for smoking, for swearing, for yelling, for arguing with umps or even fighting with other coaches or parents. The bottom line of being a parent or a coach of young ballplayers is that it is all about them and not a whit about us.

(If you drink or smoke or swear, don't be embarrassed. Join a slow-pitch softball league or go bowling and get it out of your system. Just keep that stuff away from the kids. They'll discover it all soon enough on their own.)

Using Everything We've Got

To be successful as parents and coaches of young baseball players, we are going to have to talk their language about their game. This only makes sense, considering it is easier for adults to adjust our language than it is for them to adjust theirs. This requires that we spend time listening to our kids, observing their reactions to things and how they communicate with each other. Once we learn their "buzz words" and "hot buttons," effective dialogue and instruction is sure to follow.

Look at children when you are talking to them. Are they soaking in everything you say? Those are the "sponges." Are they looking at the ground, watching butterflies, or playing with their gloves while your words bounce right off them? These are the "rocks." What's the most noticeable difference between rocks and sponges? Good eye contact for starters. When we're coaching or instructing kids we have to make good eye contact with them and demand good eye contact from them. Their eyes are the passageways to their ears. Equally as important, maintaining good eye contact is an excellent lesson in showing respect for others. Learning it will be something kids will benefit from for the rest of their lives.

Still, we've got to factor in that young people's attention spans are naturally much shorter than ours. In fact, we may only have a small window of time in which to actually instruct them, so we must keep our coaching simple, enthusiastic and brief. At this age, listening will be one of their least favorite activities. We may hold their attention a little longer by changing speakers (let the assistant coaches or other parents join in) or by making instruction interactive and letting them ask questions, make comments, or share their thoughts on what you just said. But even then there will be a limit. Once you go past it you are wasting valuable time—yours and theirs. That's when it's time to stop coaching and just let them play the game.

Helping Kids Exceed Their Personal Comfort Level

Our goal as parents and coaches of young players is to help them get comfortable with the great game of baseball—its ups, downs, challenges, duties, responsibilities, commitments, etc. At that point, they can start having fun and performing on the field. But what happens when they have found that comfort level? Do we declare, "job well done," and leave it at that? Or do we encourage them to challenge themselves to continue to grow: "You're good, and you could be even better." This is a delicate matter for any parent or coach.

One method of escalating young athletes' comfort level is to offer a challenge to their talent. Let them compete with older and better players. Increase the number or quality of the leagues they play in. This will allow them to discover their own weaknesses and begin working on them. Take kids to high school or college games and let them observe what players are doing at the next level. Let them get used to the size and skill of their

A True Story

Here's a story about using our legs to help us get our ears to work properly. I was a high school baseball coach for nine years. During that period I always caught myself saying, "Didn't you learn that in tee-ball?" And I was always amazed that they hadn't.

When my own kids started playing tee-ball, I knew that I had to practice what I preached. At our first practice, I had the kids gather around me and we all sat down on the grass in order to go through the rules for the team. "Welcome," I said, "this is your first year playing the greatest game ever invented, and here is what we are going to do. Rule number one: We are going to have fun. Rule number two: We are going to learn how to hit and catch...."

"Oops, Jeff," I said to one of the boys who was giggling with a friend, "now is a good time to learn rule number three: We are going to learn how to pay attention. So, when I am talking, I should be the only one talking, that way we can all learn the stuff we need to know. See the backstop over there?" I pointed to one that was about fifty feet from where we were sitting. "If somebody talks while I am talking, everyone on the team will have to run over there and back as fast as you can. Okay?"

Everyone nodded.

"Okay. Rule number four...." About that time another kid whispered to his buddy. "Okay, everyone to the backstop," I said. All of the kids jumped up laughing and ran to the backstop. When they returned I said about three more words before they had to run again, still giggling. After about the sixth trip to the screen, however, the kids were shushing each other to keep quiet.

They didn't have to run very far, but they soon learned that I needed their attention before we could get to the really cool stuff like hitting and catching. I never had to raise my voice that year, and the lesson was learned very early. In return, I made sure I kept my talks short and kept all my players active working on the "cool stuff," to make sure I never forgot or lost track of rule number one!

future competition. Then, start instilling positive thoughts and positive talk to overcome ungrounded fears. Remember one thing we do have absolute control over is our thoughts. Continuously express your confidence in their ability to achieve their goals.

If we have successfully taught our children that "I can't" or "I quit" are not acceptable options or solutions, being able to challenge them to improve and work harder will be much easier. Once they accept the challenge to elevate their game, they will usually stay with it until they actually succeed. The early training we gave them will pay some big dividends at this point in their baseball careers. We will have successfully taught them to overcome adversity and make the adjustments necessary to accomplish what they set out to do.

Properly Preparing Children for the Next Level

Early on in baseball, genetics are not a major factor. However, as a ballplayer continues to advance from one level to the next, his or her height, weight, speed and strength start to become more and more important. We have to be able to help kids make realistic choices and decisions, such as changing positions or possibly even getting into a different sport that is more conducive to their strengths and skills. We may need to enroll them in clinics and camps to improve their skills and mechanics. We may also have to get them into specialized strength, flexibility and conditioning programs. However, knowing that moving up to the next level means added pressures, expectations, time commitments, and tougher or more experienced competition, it is important that we adults assist them in making a realistic assessment of both their goals and ability to achieve them.

Studies show that nearly seventy percent of all children playing any kind of youth sport drop out of their sports programs entirely by age fifteen. When surveyed and interviewed privately regarding their decision to quit, these young people site several reasons for losing interest and no longer having fun. Among these are:

- Fear of failure or inability to achieve and sustain success.
- Fear of public failure or humiliation.
- Fear of disappointing their parents.
- Fear of verbal abuse by coaches or fans.
- Fear of injury.

These are all red flags that we parents and coaches must constantly be on the lookout for as our children mature. Children's fears, anxieties and concerns about competition, expectations and pressures should be addressed, discussed and put to rest early on in their sports career. This assurance and comforting process will be ongoing as new pressures, concerns and fears arise as they continue to climb in their sports careers.

What Every High School and College Coach Is Looking for in a "Prospect"

Here are a few of the qualities and skills that high school and college coaches look for in a student baseball player, according to Regis Tremblay of the Center for Kids First in Sports:

- A player with a strong work ethic and healthy desire to succeed.
- A player who is not selfish and will do what is best for his team when asked to by his coach.
- A player with good leadership qualities.
- A player that gives 100% effort on the practice field and in games.
- A player with sound moral character, respect for his teammates, and a positive attitude.

By the way, if any of these sound familiar, they should. These are some of the life skills that we have professed throughout this entire book. It is no coincidence that coaches look for these same qualities in upper-level prospects. All coaches know that these types of players tend to make their teams good and their teammates better.

TEACH YOUR

Avoid alcohol, tobacco and drugs. These things can only hurt you and will never help you.

PLAYERS THIS

Life Skills Learning Drill 25

"The Strikeout Drill"

This drill teaches children that maintaining their pride and poise after a setback is so important that it is worth practicing until perfected.

If kids play baseball long enough, two things are inevitable: They are going to strike out a lot and they are not going to like it. Eventually, somebody on the team is going to come back to the dugout and throw his or her bat or helmet or both. This leads to even more bad habits that escalate in magnitude and grandeur if left unchecked. So at the very beginning of the season, run the strikeout drill. At one of the first team practices, get the team all together with their helmets on and bats in hand at the on deck circle. One at a time they will practice going to the plate, swinging and missing, hustling back to the dugout, and politely putting their helmet and bat away and sitting on the bench. When they are all back on the bench, start the drill over again. Finally, one of them will realize the point of the drill and will beg to stop. Then you can agree to stop for now, but promise to repeat the drill when anyone acts foolishly after striking out.

Life Skills Learning Drill 26

"Tag Team Coaching"

This drill emphasizes the importance of adults teaching skills to other people's children—whether they are baseball skills or skills for the ballgame of life.

Ask a group of dads or moms (two or more) to show up on any given practice day. Have the parents meet with each other and the coach before the practice begins. Assign each parent to a player or players other than his or her own. Tell each parent what exact skill should be worked on and what drills to use to do so. Kids will be receptive to someone new showing interest in them. They will listen to another parent and take suggestions much more readily than if their own parent made them, even using the exact same words. Then on the way home each parent can ask what had been learned from "Tommy's dad" or "Mary's mom" at practice. This conversation will also allow the parent to positively get two cents in on the subject and reinforce the lesson. Parents and coaches can all exchange ideas and feedback at the next practice or game.

Life Skills Learning Drill 27

"Beat the Stopwatch Drill"

This drill emphasizes being able to perform well under time constraints. This is a very valuable skill in baseball and in life. This drill also teaches children to handle pressure in situations where time is critical.

Keep increasing the pace and speed of all your drills. Whatever a young ballplayer is doing well, he or she needs to do it faster. This includes everything from bat speed, to arm speed, to running speed, to speed in catching and releasing the ball. Start working with a stopwatch. The goal is for children to maintain the good mechanics but do everything just a little quicker. Make them comfortable with the idea of being timed. It will soon become a challenge for them, and they will enjoy breaking their own "best times" when doing drills.

Extra Innings

Ten Commitments by Parents and Coaches

To ensure the happiness, success and well-being of all our young baseball players, we coaches and parents make the following ten commitments:

Commitment Number One: *We will use sports to teach and reinforce the personal skills and moral qualities that give our young ballplayers the greatest opportunity to succeed in life.*

Commitment Number Two: *We will be positive and upbeat role models first and coaches/fans second, because what we teach our young ballplayers with our own kind conduct, well-chosen words, and measured reactions have a far more lasting impact on them than anything we teach them about a game.*

Commitment Number Three: *We will create a fun and supportive environment that allows our young ballplayers to learn, develop and refine (through both success and failure) a good work ethic and a sense of confidence in their ability to achieve.*

Commitment Number Four: *We will make a regular habit of saying, "We're proud of you," to our young ballplayers. We will tell them this when they do something exceptionally well and even when they don't. We will always remember that children are happiest and most productive when they know they are loved and appreciated unconditionally.*

Commitment Number Five: *We will take it as our personal responsibility to help our young ballplayers overcome their frustrations and disappointments as they arise. We will avoid, at all costs, heaping any of our own frustrations or disappointments on them.*

Commitment Number Six: *We will patiently turn those situations where our young ballplayers proclaim "I can't" or "I quit" into proclamations of "I can" and "I will." We will accomplish this by calmly acknowledging their frustrations, talking and working through their anxieties, and setting up opportunities for them to successfully overcome their fears and failings.*

Commitment Number Seven: *We will accept the challenge of modeling for our young ballplayers the qualities, characteristics and traits necessary for them to become good leaders...for their team and for the world.*

Commitment Number Eight: *We will teach our young ballplayers good listening and learning skills by being good listeners ourselves. We will spend time learning from and listening to them and offer them good reasons and motivation to listen and learn from us.*

Commitment Number Nine: *We will help our young ballplayers make honest and realistic assessments of their personal abilities, skills and talents. We will help them make the logical and appropriate choices when choosing from their options and will give them the support, encouragement and as-*

sistance they need to succeed once they have made their own decisions and set their own goals.

Commitment Number Ten: *We will constantly remind ourselves that we are never too old to learn to be a better parent, coach, or role model for our young ballplayers. For their sake, as well as for our own, we will do so!*

Post-Game

Acknowledgments

First of all, let us both thank Peter Gammons for writing the Foreword to this book. It is an honor to have a Hall of Famer think that what we have to say to coaches and parents of young baseball players has value.

Joe and Dave

Mom, thanks for all the unconditional love you gave me in between the home runs and strikeouts of my life. You never waivered. You celebrated me through the good and the bad. I also want to thank you for teaching me how to play the game of life correctly. I could not have asked for or had more wonderful parents than you and Dad. I am grateful to you both and love you more than you can know.

Tanner Rylee Smith, I owe you everything for letting me experience the unparalleled joys of fatherhood. I only hope I can be half as good a parent to you as your Grandma Delores and Grandpa Merlyn were to me. You were my Super Star from the minute you were born, and that will never change.

Kathleen, you have always been the one. I appreciated your encouragement and willingness to let me disappear for hours on end to write this book. (And Shirley, thanks for giving me a place to disappear to.) Stan, the brother I never had, thanks for your advice, friendship, honesty and input (both in this book and in my life). Coach Rutschman, Coach Arbuckle, Geno—your wisdom, confidence, and "humility lessons" have been immeasurably helpful.

And Joey, all my clients have been like sons to me. You just happened to be one of my favorite sons. It was a pleasure having all those breakfast meetings at Cappy's over the years, talking baseball, fatherhood, spirituality, and life's many challenges. Who would have thought all those conversations would have ended up in this book? You're a good friend, Joe, and I can't thank you enough for that friendship.

David Allen Smith
Newport Beach, California

Big Joe, you have been a great father and grandfather, and you were the best coach I ever had. Thanks for the time you spent with me both on and off the baseball field and for teaching me life's most important lessons. May I pass your patience and teaching ability on to Tripp and Travis as they grow up. You are the Man! Ma, thanks for your support as you sat through countless games and washed many dirty uniforms.

Tripp and Travis, it is a joy to watch the two of you play baseball. I hope this book helps the two of you not make the same mistakes that I have made; and I pray that the time we have spent together on the baseball field will prove as fruitful for you as it already has for me. I love you guys.

To the Chief, my beautiful wife, thanks for always supporting me and for being my biggest fan. We have had some unbelievable times traveling to all ends of this country chasing a game, and you have made every place we have lived feel like home. May God bless us as we do it again with our boys. Thanks for your dedication and for being the glue in our wonderful marriage.

Dave Magadan, Davey Lopes, Joe Pettini, Carlos Tosca, Jeff Pentland, Smokey Garrett, and Ron LaRuffa—you have been the best coaches to be coached by and to coach with. Thanks for finding something in me to believe in and for the vast amount of knowledge about baseball you have shared with me.

Dave, all those breakfasts at Cappy's finally amounted to something. Thank you for being a great friend, above and beyond being a super agent. You are a first-round draft pick.

Finally, thank you Heavenly Father, without whom none of this would have been possible, and for the provisions you have made for us through your Son, Jesus Christ. Our deepest thanks belong to you for the talents, abilities and blessings you have bestowed upon our lives. To you be the glory.

Joseph Aversa, Jr.
Fountain Valley, California

Box Score

"True Story" Bylines

True Story on page 21: Submitted by Stan Manley
True Story on page 34: Submitted by Paul Weaver
True Story on page 45: Submitted by Dave Smith
True Story on page 54: Submitted by Stan Manley
True Story on page 64: Submitted by Joe Aversa
True Story on page 76: Submitted by Jean Larkin
True Story on page 88: Submitted by Dave Smith
True Story on page 98: Submitted by Greg Pierce
True Story on page 110: Submitted by Stan Manley

All stories were used with permission.

Other Baseball Books from ACTA Sports

THE LIFE OF LOU GEHRIG
Told by a Fan
Sara Kaden Brunsvold
A new biography of the great Yankees' first baseman that covers his life from start to finish, while always being careful to highlight the human stories from his life that fill in the gaps between the facts, such as his cures for hitting slumps, his favorite foods, and even his attempt at comedy. 256 pages, paperback, $14.95

DIAMOND PRESENCE
Twelve Stories of Finding God at the Old Ball Park
Edited by Gregory F. Augustine Pierce
A touching collection of twelve true, short stories in which the authors relate how they came to feel the presence of God while enjoying the great American pastime of baseball as players, coaches, parents, children or just plain fans. 176 pages, hardcover, $17.95

STRAT-O-MATIC FANATICS
The Unlikely Success Story of a Game That Became an American Passion
Glenn Guzzo
This is the true story behind the creation—and re-creation—of America's most popular sports board game ever: Strat-O-Matic. This book looks at the hobby from every angle: the numerous crises that nearly engulfed the small company as well as fascinating anecdotes from real players of the game. 320 pages, paperback, $14.95

Available from booksellers or call (800) 397-2282
www.actasports.com

More Standing Ovations for *The Ballgame of Life*

As a kid learning the game of baseball and dreaming of making it to the major leagues, I always knew there was something special going on between those chalk lines that was far more important than how far I could hit or how hard I could throw. The Ballgame of Life *beautifully captures what is so special about teaching the game of baseball to kids. Every mom, dad, aunt, uncle and coach needs to read this book and follow its philosophy to the letter.*

—Kevin Millar, Major League Ballplayer

Absolutely hits the mark! If there were one book I could get my parents and coaches to read, it would be The Ballgame of Life.

—Mike Herrera, President, Fountain Valley Little League

Whether it is for the tips, the drills, the stories, or the sound philosophy, share this book with every parent or coach you know or meet. They will not stop thanking you.

—Gene Manley, Member, Fast Pitch Softball Hall of Fame

If all adults treated others the way my five-year-old's tee-ball team treats one another, we would have better communities and a better world. This is the practical wisdom of The Ballgame of Life.

—Jim Torrey, Former Mayor, Eugene, Oregon;
Executive Director, Eugene–Springfield Kidsports

If adults are going to participate in youth baseball in any capacity, they need to bring something positive, productive and rewarding to the game. The Ballgame of Life *tells exactly what that "something" is.*

—Jim Dedrick, Major League Player
and Private Pitching Instructor